C000257472

PETRA

AN ARCHAEOLOGICAL GUIDE

Wojciech Machowski

Translated by Ian Jenkins

Cover and interior design by Karolina Kawecka

First Edition

ISBN: 978-83-935757-0-1

www.archaeoguides.com

CONTENTS

Introduction.. 5
History of Petra and the Nabataeans.. 9
The History of Archaeological Research at the Petra Site 25
The Façade Tombs.. 29
The Gods of the Nabataeans.. 37
Practical Information.. 45
Trail 1 51
Trail 2 85
Trail 3 105
Trail 4 115
Trail 5 131
Trail 6 147
Trail 7 155
Trail 8 171
Trail 9 179
Trail 10.. 187
Trail 11.. 195
Glossary 203
Selected bibliography 206

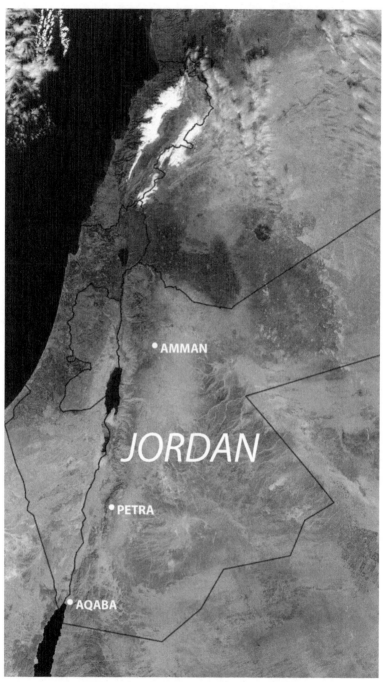

Fig. 1 – Satellite map of Jordan with the position of Petra (Source: NASA).

INTRODUCTION

Petra is located in the southern part of modern day Jordan, approximately 80km to the south of the Dead Sea **(Fig. 1)**.

It lies amidst steep cliffs on the eastern side of the Wadi Araba, part of the great tectonic structure known as the Syrian-African Rift. This geographical feature, which came into being 300 million years ago, traverses the territory from southern Turkey all the way to North Africa and forms a natural border between Palestine to the west and the territories of Transjordan to the east **(Fig. 2)**.

Fig. 2 – The eastern slope of the Wadi Araba, the place where the Nabataeans built their capital city of Petra. The view is from Jabal Haroon.

Strabo, a Greek historian of the 1st century CE, first made mention of the exceptional location of Petra, stressing the extremely inhospitable nature of its surroundings:

The capital of the Nabataeans is called Petra (the Rock). It is situated on a spot, which is surrounded and fortified by a smooth and level rock, which externally is abrupt and precipitous, but within there are abundant springs of water both for domestic purposes and for watering gardens. Beyond the enclosure the country is for the most part a desert, particularly towards Judea (Geog. 16.4.21).

Fig. 3 – The Wadi Musa (Valley of Moses) and the ancient city of Petra. View from the top of Umm al-Biyara.

Strabo did not err from the truth. Petra is situated within the extensive Wadi Musa (Valley of Moses), which lies between the imposing rock elevations of Umm al-Biyara and al-Khubtha **(Fig. 3)**. The site is additionally secured to the north by the near inaccessible M'eisrah Mountains and the Mughar an-Nasara elevation, whilst the steep (but flat at the summit) Jabal Madbah rises to the south-east. The latter was not only the site of an important Nabataean religious centre (the High Place of Sacrifice), but also an excellent observation point, as from here it was possible to monitor all the territory to the south and east of Petra. Further to the east is the impressive Shara Massif (referred to in the Bible as 'Seir'). Various springs can be found around the massif, including the Ayn Musa ('Moses' Well'). These ensured a year-round supply of fresh water adequate to meet the needs of the population of Petra and its few cultivated areas.

An undoubted attribute of the site was its location near to the meeting point of two of the most important caravan routes of the Near East, namely the Silk Road (linking China and the Persian Gulf to Egypt) and the Spice Route (linking southern Arabia to Damascus and the Mediterranean). From Petra itself, yet another caravan route began, cutting across the Wadi Araba and Negev desert and leading directly to the ports of the Mediterranean (such as Gaza and Rhinocolura), from where goods could be sent on to the very lucrative markets of Ancient Rome. Goods from southern Arabia and the further distant India and China, such as iron, copper, gold, silk, spices, incense, perfume and ivory all passed through Petra. The city was thus extraordinarily well positioned to exercise control over the far-reaching caravan trade and to draw huge profits from it.

The word "petra" means 'rock' in Greek. The name was used by various ancient authors and also appeared in its Hebrew version, "Sela". We also know from inscriptions, as well as biblical passages (e.g. Numbers 31.8 or Joshua 13.21), that the Semitic name of the city was "Reqem" (or Raqmu), which means 'many-coloured'.

Fig. 4 – The mighty rock of "as-Sela".

The surroundings of Petra were inhabited by humans as early as the Stone Age, starting in the Lower Palaeolithic period (around 300,000 years ago). In the Neolithic period (8500-4500 BCE), an important settlement developed in the Wadi Beidha, the archaeological remains of which can be viewed during a trip to Siq al-Barid, also known as 'Little Petra'. According to the Old Testament (Genesis 36.20.29; Deuteronomy 2.12.22), the region was then inhabited by Horites in the Bronze Age (approx. 3200-1200 BCE). Israelites were later to appear in the Petra area, led by Moses from Egypt on their way to the Promised Land. The memory of these events is preserved in local geographical names such as the abovementioned Ayn Musa (Moses' Well) and Jabal an-Nabi Haroon (Mount Aaron). The former is the place where, according to legend, Moses caused a spring to appear by striking a rock with his staff, while the second is the place where Moses' deceased brother, Aaron, was laid to rest.

In the Iron Age (1200-539 BCE), the Petra region was settled, along with all of southern Transjordan, by the Edomites, who are referred to in the Old Testament as the descendants of Esau and fierce enemies of the Israelites (Genesis 36). The remains of cities from this period have been discovered at nearby Tawilan and at the summit of the Umm al-Biyara rock (which towers over central Petra), as well as at other sites. Tawilan was a large fortified settlement and dates mainly to the 7th and 6th centuries BCE, whereas the site at the peak of Umm al-Biyara mainly contained the remains of houses and a series of cisterns. The latter collected water and also gave the site its name, the 'Mother of Cisterns' ("Umm al-Biyara" in Arabic). The capital of the land of the Edomites was Bosorah (present day Buseirah), located 50km to the north of Petra. The mighty rock of "as-Sela" **(Fig. 4)** is in the vicinity and is thought to be the place described in the Old Testament as Sela ('rock'), where King Amaziah slaughtered 10,000 Edomites (II Chronicles 25.11-12).

In the 6th century BCE, the Edomites were defeated by the Babylonian king, Nabonidus (556-539 BCE), and the vast majority of them were subsequently deported to Babylon. Groups of nomads began to flow into the now deserted lands, amongst whom the Nabataeans took centre stage. Archaeological research has demonstrated that there was no military aggression involved and that a gradual and peaceful process of integration took place instead. As a result, there was a degree of cultural continuation between the time of the Edomites and that of the Nabataeans.

We do not know for sure from whence the Nabataeans emerged nor from whom they were descended. They could have been merchants, shepherds or even desert bandits and they may either have previously had a fixed abode or pursued a nomadic existence, as was the case with so many other tribes of the region. These doubts have led to the creation of many differing theories concerning the origins of the Nabataeans.

Certain researchers believe that they were descended from the biblical character of Nebaioth, the first son of Ishmael (Genesis 25.13). According to an interesting hypothesis of A. Knauf based on the name of Ishmael (one of the sons of Abraham), the term could cover a confederation of Arab tribes who were described in the Bible as his descendants. If this were the case, Genesis (the book containing the information) could give us a description of the ethnic situation in the desert areas lying between Egypt and Mesopotamia in the 8th and 7th centuries BCE. The Nabataeans would thus be one of the described nomadic peoples living in the desert and perhaps could have created their own kind of confederation in an area which must have lain somewhere to the east of the Wadi Araba.

Another closely related theory suggests that the Nabataeans were part of the tribal confederation of the Qedarites (Qedar was also the name of one of the sons of Ishmael), well-known from other sources of material from the 8th and 7th centuries BCE. According to this theory, the Nabataean people would have resided in southern Transjordan and would have become the dominant political power during the period of Persian domination (after 539 BCE). The Nabataeans would have then taken control of the already long-standing Qedar tribal confederation and independently created their own state with Petra as its capital.

Many contemporary researchers take a critical view of such theories and instead make reference to other sources of information on the Nabataeans. Assyrian tablets in cuneiform script, for example, bear the names of tribes called the Nabatu and Nabayati. Another example is an inscription from the 6th century BCE, discovered near the Tayma oasis, which informs us of a war waged against the Nabayati people. It is therefore probable that they were a highly mobile nomadic tribe, which would explain why it is possible to discover them in sources from different time periods from the south of the whole Fertile Crescent region. This, in turn, poses great difficulties to archaeologists trying to identify them, since these nomads did not build fixed abodes or model pots and the slight traces left by their settlements long ago disappeared into the desert sand.

Yet despite all these difficulties, the search for traces of the first Nabataeans goes on and new possible solutions to the mystery continue to appear.

The traditional view of researchers is that the Nabataeans came from southern Arabia, the area seen as the cradle of many Arab peoples. In approximately the 6th century BCE, they would have then moved from here to the north along caravan routes to occupy the areas previously inhabited by the Edomites.

Another theory has the Nabataeans coming from the territories of north-eastern Arabia. On the basis of the epigraphic evidence mentioned above, some researchers have attempted to link their origins to the al-Hufuf region (near the island of Bahrain) and the territories of southern Mesopotamia. A key element of this hypothesis are Assyrian annuals from the period of Tiglath-Pileser III's rule (745-729 BCE), which listed the Nabatu among 36 rebellious tribes living somewhere between the central Euphrates and lower Tigris rivers. In 703 BCE, the Nabatu people were again mentioned, this time as one of the opponents of the Sennacherib (704-681 BCE) during their war with the Chaldeans. The presence of nomads in the region of southern Babylon has been further confirmed by inscriptions discovered at sites such as Ur, Uruk and Nippur and their traces are also still visible in the central Euphrates region and on the coast of the Persian Gulf. We also know that between the years 641 to 638 BCE, a Qedarite leader by the name of Abiyate, in coalition with a certain Natnu (the leader of the Nabayati people), attacked the western border of the Assyrian Empire from the Syrian Desert.

All the epigraphic evidence connected to the Nabataeans discovered thus far has one common failing – none of it states where the Nabatu or Nabayati lived. This could be because they were a nomadic tribe without a fixed residence who acted as middle-men in trade, watched over the caravan routes running through the desert and from time to time appeared in documents left by settled tribes, for example those of the territories of Mesopotamia. Therefore, it seems safest to treat the vast deserts within the Fertile Crescent as the birthplace of the Nabataean civilisation and the Nabataeans themselves as one of the nomadic tribes originally living somewhere between Egypt and Mesopotamia. They may have been one, continuously wandering tribe or they may have been several different ones with similar names, a theory which would explain the present day confusion over their origins.

Nevertheless, it is certain that, by the end of the 6th century BCE, the Nabataeans were already well-organised and that they had created the foundations of a powerful, independent political kingdom with Petra as its capital. However, as they were still nomads, they did not permanently reside at Petra at once. It was only later, after fully appreciating the worth of the site, that they chose it to be one of their permanent settlements.

It has not yet been proven that the Nabataeans erected any permanent, stone buildings in either the 6th or 5th centuries BCE. The first archaeological traces only emerge at the end of the 4th century BCE, a period only a little before the invasion of the Macedonians. This event was described by Diodorus Siculus, a Greek historian who lived in the second half of the 1st century BCE. Using an eyewitness account written by Hieronymus of Cardia (a Greek officer who served in Palestine at the end of the 4th century BCE) which managed to survive until his time, Diodorus was able to describe the first historical events in which the Nabataeans participated in his *Bibliotheca Historica* (Bibl. 19. 95. 1-2).

In about 312-311 BCE, Antigonous the One-Eyed, a leader of the Macedonian Antigonid dynasty, ordered one of his commanders by the name of Athenaeus to seize valuable goods which were being kept by the Nabataeans at the summit of a rock which was difficult to access. Both of them knew that the Nabataeans celebrated a kind of holiday every year (maybe a festival or fair) in which only the men took part. At this time, elderly men, women and children were left with all the Nabataean possessions on top of a steep, naturally fortified rock. This rock had only one narrow path leading to the summit, making it easy to defend. Although it is certainly possible, we cannot be certain that this description refers to the mighty Umm al-Biyara rock which towers over Petra. Indeed, certain researchers believe that it pertains to the as-Sela summit, which lies approximately 50km to the north of Petra, the same site where Amaziah slaughtered the Edomites.

A Greek army numbering 4,000 infantry and 600 riders thus moved out of the territories of Palestine and, after three days of marching, reached the rock fortress. Under the cover of darkness, the Greeks climbed to the summit, murdered many of the people staying there and took the rest into slavery. They then began their return journey bearing an enormous amount of stolen incense and myrrh as well as about 500 talents of silver. They were not to reach Antigonous, however, as news of the sneak attack quickly reached the Nabataeans, who immediately gave chase. On catching the Greek army, a brutal bloodbath ensued which saw Athenaeus killed with all of his soldiers, save for about 50 who managed to escape.

After returning to their settlement, the Nabataeans sent a letter to Antigonous (written in Aramaic) complaining of his surprise attack. The humiliated Antigonous replied diplomatically that it was Athenaeus and not he who was responsible for the attack and that his commander had ignored orders and attacked of his own volition. Nevertheless, Antigonous was soon to send another army to attack the Nabataeans, this time commanded by his own son, Demetrius, who went by the name of *"Poliorketes"* ('the Besieger'). This time, however, the Arabs learned of the Greek attack in advance and were able to prevent it by sending emissaries to Demetrius to persuade him to accept a payment in return for retreating towards the Dead Sea.

In the beginning, at the turn of the 4th and 3rd centuries BCE, Petra only developed slowly. Diodorus Siculus was able to shed some light on what life would have been like. According to his account, the Nabataeans at this time still lived in tents rather than in proper houses and pursued a semi-nomadic lifestyle, a fact which has now been confirmed by archaeological research at Petra, mainly within the framework of the Early Petra Project.

As for sustenance, the Nabataeans consumed meat, milk and plants, all of which they produced and grew themselves. Apart from this, they also collected 'wild honey' from the trees, which they then imbibed after mixing it with water. Consumption of wine was forbidden. They stored their riches in fairly inaccessible places, most often on the peaks of rocks which were easy to defend, such as Umm al-Biyara in Petra.

In Siculus' account, the Nabataean people numbered only 10,000, but were the wealthiest of the Arab tribes. This affluence mainly resulted from the trading of incense, myrrh and the most valuable root spices, which were supplied by the regions of southern Arabia (known as Arabia Felix, meaning 'Fortunate Arabia', present day Yemen). The Nabataeans also greatly profited from the selling of bitumen from the asphalt mines of the Dead Sea to the Egyptians, who used it to embalm corpses.

Diodorus additionally expressed his admiration for the Nabataean skill in collecting water. As the land was bereft of natural sources of water, they dug deep cisterns, which filled with water during the rainy season. The existence and location of these cisterns was a closely guarded secret, so as to prevent invading foreign armies from making use of them. As a result, enemies who attacked but were unaware of the hidden water stores very often died of thirst. Diodorus went on to claim that this was also the reason why the Nabataeans were able to remain independent, despite the attacks of mighty armies. First it was the Assyrians who failed to enslave them. Then it was the turn of the Medeans, the Persians and finally the Macedonians. Nobody was able to subjugate them to their rule.

After this relatively early account of the customs and lifestyle of the Nabataeans, there is a relatively long period during which there are no reliable historical reports concerning them. The next information which we possess comes from the rule of the first Nabataean king who we know by name. He was called Haretat, but he is better known by his Greek name, Aretas I.

Aretas I (second quarter of the 2nd century BCE)

An event which occurred during the reign of Aretas I is related in the Second Book of Maccabees, in which we learn that Jason, the High Priest of Jerusalem, was accused and imprisoned by Aretas, the king of the Nabataeans (2 Maccabees 5.8). However, aside from the fact that Aretas was in power around 168 BCE, which is also confirmed by inscriptions discovered close to the city of Elusa in the Negev, we know nothing more about him.

During this period (the 2nd century BCE), the Nabataeans led a relatively peaceful existence in the desert lands to the east of the River Jordan and the Wadi Araba. They maintained peaceful relations with their neighbours, although this was mainly because they all shared one common enemy, the Seleucids. However, the situation began to change at the end of the century.

Aretas II (120/110 – 96 BCE)

According to an account of Titus Flavius Josephus, a Jewish historian, we know that in about 100 BCE, Jannaeus, a king of the Hasmonaean dynasty (also known as Alexander), defeated Gaza, a city which was allied to the Nabataeans. Its inhabitants had counted on the support of Aretas (this time Aretas II rather than Aretas I), but he did not come to their aid (AJ 13.13.3). After the capture of Gaza, previously the main port of the Nabataeans on the Mediterranean, military encounters became more and more commonplace between the Jewish Hasmonaeans and the Arab Nabataeans. As a result of these battles, the Nabataeans lost a total of twelve cities from Madaba in Moab (Jordan) all the way to Elusa in the northern Negev (Israel).

Obodas I (96 – 85 BCE) and Rabbel I (approx. 85 BCE)

The successor of Aretas II was his son, Obodas. According to Josephus (BJ 1.4.4), he exacted his revenge on Alexander Jannaeus by defeating him in battle at Garada in about 93 BCE. This did not, however, aid the Nabataeans in their quest to retake the twelve cities previously lost to the Hasmonaean leader.

We also know from Josephus (BJ 1.4.7; AJ 13.15.1) that, in about 85 BCE, the leader of Syria from the Seleucid dynasty, Antiochus XII Dionysus, undertook two expeditions against the Nabataeans. We know virtually nothing of the first, apart from the fact that he was forced to put it on hold in order to return to Damascus to reassert his rule. A little later he once again led his army south, but this time the end was tragic. He died in battle and his army was vanquished. Shortly afterwards, the Nabataeans took Damascus.

For the moment, it remains a mystery which Nabataean leader defeated Antiochus XII. Was it Obodas I, who died shortly after the battle, perhaps because of the wounds he had sustained? Or was it his brother, Rabbel I, who reigned briefly around 85 BCE, as has been attested by inscriptions discovered by archaeologists?

Aretas III (84 – 62/61 BCE)

If you study Flavius Josephus' account of Antiochus' campaign in Arabia very carefully, it is also possible to come to the conclusion that the man who defeated him was the son of Obodas I, Aretas. The historian writes (BJ 1.4.8; AJ 13.15.2) that, at the behest of its citizens, Aretas took over kingly duties in Damascus after the death of Antiochus XII. It is difficult to imagine that the residents of Damascus would have chosen an inexperienced youth who had just acceded to the Nabataean throne to defend their city. It is more probable that they realised that after his victory over Antiochus XII (an outcome feared for good reason by Alexander Jannaeus), Aretas III had become the most powerful leader in the region. The governance of such a monarch, who in addition was king of a country which lived off commerce and trade, would have seemed to be a guarantee of peace and affluence to the residents of Damascus, a city which was also located on a trade route.

The beginning of a long-lasting political and geographical heyday for the Nabataean state accompanied the advent of Aretas III's rule. Between 84 and 72 BCE, Aretas III struck coins in Damascus which bore his name and the moniker of *Philhellenos* ('lover of Greek culture'). However, just after 72 BCE, the Nabataeans withdrew from Damascus, leaving it in the hands of the Armenian king, Tigranes.

In the later period of his rule, Aretas III involved himself in the power struggle for Judaea between Hyrcanus II and Aristobulus, who were both sons of Alexander Jannaeus. After losing a decisive battle at Jericho, Hyrcanus was prompted by his advisor, Antipater (who was of Idumaean descent and married to a Nabataean by the name of Kypron), to seek the assistance of Aretas. After Hyrcanus had agreed to give back the twelve cities taken by his father, Aretas decided to assist him. They quickly dealt with the armies of Aristobulus and proceeded to lay siege to Jerusalem. However, Aretas was forced to desist from further battles when the Romans appeared in Judaea. At this time, Marcus Aemilius Scaurus, one of Pompey the Great's generals, received legations from both Aristobulus (who successfully bribed him) and Hyrcanus. As a result, he advised Aretas to retreat, threatening that he would consider him an enemy of Rome if he did not. Aretas did not want to risk a conflict with Rome and therefore withdrew from Palestine.

In 64 BCE, Pompey took Damascus and proceeded to acquire Jerusalem a year later, placing Hyrcanus on the throne. He then returned to Rome, leaving power in the hands of the first governor of the newly created province of Syria, the abovementioned Marcus Aemilius Scaurus. After hearing of the wealth of the Nabataeans, Scaurus wasted no time in leading an expedition to Petra. However, since access to the capital of the Nabataeans was far from straightforward, the expedition only just managed to avoid ending in complete catastrophe. Out of provisions and occupying inhospitable terrain bereft of water, Scaurus' army could easily have fallen victim to the Arabs of the region. The Nabataeans, however, were not interested in beginning a war with Rome. Once again using the services of Antipater, they instead offered Scaurus 300 talents of silver in return for a Roman withdrawal. Marcus Aemilius Scaurus readily agreed to the settlement and subsequently issued a silver denarius commemorating the event. On the obverse of the coin, Aretas III was pictured kneeling next to a camel (the symbol of the Nabataean caravan state) with the branch of a balsam tree in his hand **(Fig. 5)**.

Fig. 5 – Silver denarius issued by Marcus Aemilius Scaurus with King Aretas III kneeling beside a camel on the obverse.

Obodas II (62/61 – 59/58 BCE)

In around 62 BCE, Aretas III died and Obodas II most probably took to the throne for a short period of time. An inscription discovered by archaeologists informs us of this fact and a small number of coins struck during his reign have also been found.

Malichus I (59/58 – 30 BCE)

The successor of Obodas II was his son, Malichus, but we unfortunately have little information on what occurred during his relatively long period in power. We do know, however, that when Julius Caesar was waging war in Egypt in 47 BCE, the father of Herod the Great (referred to previously as Antipater) came to Caesar's assistance and that he persuaded Malichus to do likewise, a fact which is also mentioned by Caesar himself in his work entitled *De Bello Alexandrino* (1.1).

Several years later, a serious burning of bridges occurred between Malichus and Herod the Great, who had in the meantime become the king of Judaea. When Herod was forced to flee Jerusalem in 40 BCE under the threat of the

Parthian armies, Malichus (their secret ally) refused him asylum in Petra and would not return the costly family items which Antipater had previously left in safe keeping at the Nabataean court.

In spite of this, Herod managed to reach Alexandria and then Rome, where he sought the assistance he required to regain the throne of Judaea. As a result, Malichus was forced to suffer the consequences of his short-sighted policy a year later when the Romans drove the Parthians out of Palestine. The Nabataeans, as allies of the Parthians, were forced to pay a massive tribute to the victorious Romans.

Several years later, Cleopatra, the leader of Hellenistic Egypt, decided to stir up trouble between Herod and Malichus, so that they would begin a war against each other. The idea behind this was to incorporate the Arab kingdom into the Egyptian should Herod win. If he lost, she would seize Judaea instead. Her scheming led to a great battle at Diospolis from which the Judean army emerged victorious. Another battle then took place at Kanatha, a town located in Coele-Syria, in which the roles were reversed. This was largely because the local populace unexpectedly came to the aid of the Nabataeans by attacking Herod's army out of shock. Soon afterwards, they were able to enjoy victory and the heavy losses which they had inflicted on their foes with the Arabs. Herod was, however, able to save himself by escaping and then engaged in a type of hit-and-run warfare in which he constantly harried and laid waste to parts of the Nabataean kingdom.

In the spring of 31 BCE, Judaea experienced a powerful earthquake and Herod, after witnessing the massive damage sustained, offered the Nabataeans a ceasefire. This offer was rejected, however, and their emissary was killed. Soon after, a decisive battle took place in the vicinity of Philadelphia (modern day Amman in Jordan), in which the Nabataeans suffered a crushing defeat. Herod, avenging himself for his previous defeats, incorporated the land of Auranitis (Hauran, currently on the border of Syria and Jordan) into his kingdom and thereafter the Nabataeans were not able to regain it for a considerable amount of time, A little later, around the year 30 BCE, Malichus died.

Obodas III (30 – 9 BCE)

After Malichus I's death, he was replaced on the throne by his son, Obodas, who continued his father's policy of developing the kingdom's economy in a stable manner. This development was made possible largely due to the massive demand for luxury goods from India, China and southern Arabia on the Roman market. The majority of these goods arrived in Petra by caravan and were then sent onwards to the port of Rhinocolura on the Mediterranean.

The profits made from this trade were so great that the Roman Emperor Augustus decided to attempt to seize control of it himself.

With this aim in mind, he sent a military expedition to southern Arabia ("Arabia Felix") in about 26/25 BCE, which was led by the Roman Prefect of Egypt, Aelius Gallus. Its mission was to incorporate (or at the very least subjugate) this region, which seemed unimaginably rich, into the Roman Empire. The expedition turned into a complete fiasco. The Romans did manage to reach the land of the Sabeans and took many cities along the way. However, discouraged by the massive desert, a lack of water and above all the lack of expected riches, they returned to Egypt.

Strabo (Geog. 16.4.23) blamed a Nabataean by the name of Syllaeus, who performed the function of minister (or 'royal brother') in the court of Obodas III, for the failure of the campaign. According to Strabo, he tricked Gallus and led the Romans on roundabout paths through desert lands bereft of any form of life. It was, however, precisely thanks to him that the Nabataeans achieved their goal. Augustus, on learning how inhospitable and difficult to control this part of the world would be, abandoned his plans to subjugate it and left the profits from the trade of southern Arabian spices and fragrances in the hands of the Nabataeans.

Thanks to the profits gained from commerce over the course of three centuries (from the end of the 4th century BCE until the beginning of the Common Era), this nomadic tribe of little importance had now transformed itself into a vast, centralised kingdom with a strong seat of power in Petra. The previously mentioned Strabo, writing on the basis of a direct verbal account of his friend, Athenodorus (who had lived in Petra for several weeks) left us a description of the Nabataean state at the end of the 1st century BCE, during the reign of Obodas III:

Nabataea, a country with a large population and well supplied with pasturage (Geog. 16.4.18). Despite the vastness of its desert it was nevertheless a land which was: *well supplied with fruits except the olive; they use sesame-oil instead. The sheep are white-fleeced and the oxen are large, but the country produces no horses. Camels afford the service they require instead of horses* (Geog. 16.4.26). Some of the goods needed by the inhabitants were imported from other countries, but gold and silver and most of the aromatics came from the territories of the kingdom. Strabo went on to list copper, iron, saffron and purple costumes among the imported goods, as well as sculptures, paintings and architectonic decoration, which in his opinion were not executed by local artists, but brought in from outside Nabataea, almost certainly from Egyptian Alexandria.

Petra, which was constantly being developed and made more beautiful, must have made a massive impression on visitors at this time: *Their homes, through the use of stone, are costly; but, on account of peace, the cities are not walled* (Geog. 16.4.26). The capital of the Nabataean kingdom would indeed have been the very definition of a cosmopolitan trade centre in the 1ˢᵗ century BCE. With such an extensive list of trading and political partners, it was therefore inhabited by many Romans and other foreigners.

According to Strabo, the Nabataeans were also a very practical race, albeit with a love of pomp: *The Nabataeans are a sensible people, and are so much inclined to acquire possessions that they publicly fine anyone who has diminished his possessions and also confer honours on anyone who has increased them. Since they have but few slaves, they are served by their kinsfolk for the most part, or by one another, or by themselves; so that the custom extends even to their kings. They prepare common meals together in groups of thirteen persons and they have two girl-singers for each banquet. The king holds many drinking-bouts in magnificent style, but no one drinks more than eleven cupfuls, each time using a different golden cup. The king is so democratic that, in addition to serving himself, he sometimes even serves the rest himself in his turn. He often renders an account of his kingship in the popular assembly; and sometimes his mode of life is examined* (Geog. 16.4.26).

We also discover that: *Petra is always ruled by some king from the royal family; and the king has as an administrator one of his companions, who is called "brother"* (Geog. 16.4.21). Strabo was also extremely complimentary of the governance of Petra: *It is exceedingly well-governed; at any rate, Athenodorus, a philosopher and companion of mine, who has been in the city of the Petraeans, used to describe their government with admiration* (Geog. 16.4.21). Despite this, however, as was the case with Josephus, King Obodas himself was criticised for his excessive weakness and submissiveness towards his minister, the aforementioned Syllaeus: *because Obodas, the king, did not care much about public affairs, and particularly military affairs (this is a trait common to all the Arabian kings), and because he put everything in the power of Syllaeus* (Geog. 16.4.24).

The only thing which shocked Strabo was the way in which the Nabataeans treated their dead: *They have the same regard for the dead as for dung, as Heracleitus says: "Dead bodies more fit to be cast out than dung"; and therefore they bury even their kings beside dung-heaps* (Geog. 16.4.26). Strabo most probably misunderstood the burial customs of the Nabataeans or confused the similar sounding words meaning 'refuse dump' and 'tomb'. He also observed that: *They worship the sun, building an altar on the top of the house, and pouring libations on it daily and burning frankincense* (Geog. 16.4.26).

Let us return once more for a moment to the figure of Syllaeus, who Josephus (AJ 16.7.6) described as a smart and handsome young man. Syllaeus fell in love with the sister of Herod the Great, Salome, who also felt strong feelings for him. Syllaeus therefore asked Herod to let him take her as his wife. The king, however, demanded that Syllaeus first of all convert to Judaism and that only after doing this would he be allowed to marry her. Syllaeus was not able to agree to this, as he would have been stoned to death by his compatriots. Embittered by this experience, he became Herod's fiercest enemy, supporting all rebellions which rose up against him. This was relatively easy for him to do, as he was the de facto ruler of Petra.

Soon after Herod's reply, Syllaeus made his way to Rome, most probably to seek the support of the emperor for his plans to take over independent rule of the Nabataeans himself. On the way, one of his stops was in Miletus (in modern day Turkey) where an inscription left by him has been discovered: *"Royal Brother Syllaeus dedicates this to the god Dushara"*. Once in Rome, Syllaeus often complained to the emperor that Nabataea was under attack and that Herod's army was devastating and plundering the whole country. Wanting to blacken Herod's name still further in Augustus' eyes, he pointed out that Herod was trying to foment war, despite the fact that the maintenance of world peace was a desire so close to Augustus' heart. Syllaeus was so successful in convincing Augustus of his case that the emperor did not even want to speak to Herod's emissaries when they visited. Indeed, he even sent a threatening letter to Herod, warning that he would lose his friendship if he continued to act in the manner he was.

Aretas IV (9 BCE – 40 CE)

The situation was to be unexpectedly turned on its head soon after. In 9 BCE, King Obodas III died, most probably of poisoning. His successor was a certain Aeneas, who took the royal name of Aretas. Syllaeus, taking advantage of the fact that Aeneas had failed to ask for the emperor's permission before acceding to the throne at Petra, decided to deal with him in the same way as he had with Herod previously. By discrediting the new monarch in the eyes of Augustus, he hoped to seize the crown for himself.

Shortly after being crowned king, Aeneas-Aretas sent a letter to Rome with many gifts, including a gold crown, yet the emperor simply dismissed the Nabataean emissary. Aretas and Herod thus decided to join forces against their common enemy, Syllaeus. Herod sent his friend and advisor, the historian Nicolaus of Damascus, to Rome and together with Aretas' emissary they presented the Emperor Augustus with an account of the real situation in Arabia and Judaea. When the emperor asked Syllaeus to explain the facts he had been presented with, Syllaues tried and failed to persuade Augustus that he had been misled. Angry at having been tricked, the emperor condemned Syllaeus to death and made his peace with Herod. He then granted an audience to Aretas' emissary, in which he forgave the king for not waiting to receive power from the emperor, accepted the gifts he had sent and confirmed his rule. Finally, the citizens of Nabataea were able to breathe easy. Aretas IV went on to reorganise his administration and bring order to the country once more. His rule also coincided with the heyday of Nabataean art. The greatest number of Nabataean inscriptions come from this period and they mainly attest to the extensive building activity of the king, most of which occurred in Petra itself. Numismatic and epigraphic sources also inform us that Aretas IV adopted the moniker of *Philodemos* ('Lover of his People').

The peace and affluence which prevailed during Aretas IV's reign does mean, however, that we have little information concerning the Nabataeans from this period. Josephus (AJ 17.10.9) only makes mention of the assistance which Aretas gave the Romans in putting down Jewish uprisings which occurred after the death of Herod the Great in 4 BCE. Nothing is known of the next thirty years due to a total lack of source material. It is only in 27 CE that we discover that Aretas IV gave one of his daughters in marriage to the Judaean leader, Herod Antipas. Not long after, however, Herod Antipas fell madly in love with Herodias and promised her that he would divorce Aretas' daughter if she agreed to marry him. For Aretas, this was tantamount to a declaration of war. A great battle ensued, in which Herod Antipas lost his entire army. The Judaean leader then lodged a complaint with the Roman emperor, Tiberius, who ordered Vitellius, one of his generals, to bring him Aretas dead or alive. However, a war between the Romans and the Nabataeans did not occur, as the death of Emperor Tiberius in 37 CE put paid to the battle plans.

There is one other written source which mentions King Aretas IV. In his Second Letter to the Corinthians, the apostle Paul claims that a deputy of King Aretas wanted to take him captive in Damascus. This would signify that the city was in the hands of the Nabataeans during Aretas' rule, but it has not yet been possible to confirm or explain this in a satisfactory manner.

Malichus II (40 – 70 CE)

After the death of Aretas IV, his son, Malichus **(Fig. 6)**, took control of the country. Under his rule, peace and affluence continued to prevail in Nabataea. The Nabataeans, who were busy accumulating riches from the caravan trade, tried not to involve themselves in the affairs of their neighbours. They were only interested in maintaining a stable political situation in the region, something which the Romans were able to guarantee. This was why they sent their army to neighbouring Judaea to help the emperor quell anti-Roman rebellions. Their only desire at this time was to maintain peace in the region, as this was vital to their ability to profit further from trade.

Fig. 6 – Silver coin of Malichus II with King Malichus on the obverse (left) and Queen Shuqailat II on the reverse (right).

Rabbel II (70 – 106 CE)

After his death, Malichus II was succeeded by his son, Rabbel, whose mother, Queen Shuqailat II, ruled as regent for several years until he was of age. We have no descriptions of the Nabataean people from Rabbel II's reign and the only information about Rabbel II himself comes from coins and inscriptions. One of these inscriptions is from Oboda in the Negev and dates to 88 CE. From this we learn that Rabbel's title was "King of the Nabataeans, who brought life and deliverance to his people". We do not know, however, if this title was based on fact or if it was pure propaganda.

King Rabbel II is also remembered for being the monarch who moved the capital of the kingdom to Bosra, a site located in the north of the territory he ruled over. Probably soon after taking power, he began building this splendid city, to which he also moved his palace. This decision could have been taken because of the growing importance of the area on the transportation maps of the time, although some researchers see it as a result of the changing Nabataean economy, which was switching from trade to agriculture. The fertile lands of the north would have naturally been far more conducive to agriculture than the desert to the south.

The Roman and Byzantine Periods

Rabbel II was the last Nabataean leader. After his death in 106 CE, Emperor Trajan commanded the then governor of Syria, Cornelius Palma, to take control of Nabataea, which was the only independent country left in the region at the time. On the 22nd of March 106 CE, the Nabataean territories were thus incorporated into the Roman Empire. Bosra became the capital of the newly created province of Arabia and, in 114 CE, Petra was granted the title of metropolis by Trajan, meaning that it was still an important city, albeit no longer with the importance of a national capital. The annexation process was peaceful, as the Nabataeans preferred to continue in their affluent lifestyle as a Roman protectorate rather than to fight a war, especially considering that nomads of the Bedouin tribes were now attacking them with increasing regularity from the south.

Thanks to Roman patronage, Petra experienced an economic renaissance in the 2nd and 3rd centuries CE as it maintained its status as an important trading centre on the route between Arabia and Syria. This was aided by the first governor of Arabia, Claudius Severus, who built the Via Nova Traiana between the years of 111-114 CE linking Aila (modern day Aqaba) to Bosra and Damascus. The security provided by the *Pax Romana*, income from trade and the growing importance of irrigation farming all ensured the continuing development of Petra during the period of Roman rule. In 130 CE, during an inspection of his eastern provinces, Emperor Hadrian visited Petra and decided to rebuild the centre of the city to give it a more Roman character. He also granted Petra the title of *Augustocolonia Antoniana Hadriana Metropolis*.

During the reign of Emperor Constantine, who decreed Christianity to be the religion of Rome in 324 CE, Petra became the seat of a Christian bishop, although pagan cults continued to exist here for many decades after.

On the 19th of May 363 CE, a powerful earthquake struck Petra, which caused the destruction of many public buildings, many of which were never rebuilt. Despite this, Petra remained inhabited, new churches were built and those still involved in cults made use of former Nabataean tombs and temples for their spiritual needs. In the second half of the 4th century, the character of the main street of the city changed, as the colonnades which lined it on both sides were converted into shops and houses by making use of fragments of architecture taken from public buildings (such as temples) which had fallen into disuse. A series of powerful earthquakes again struck Petra in the 7th and 8th centuries and this was most probably the cause of the gradual abandonment and eventual fall of the city.

In the 12th century, a fortress (al-Wu'eira) and forts (e.g. al-Habis) built by crusaders continued to function here, but they were abandoned not long afterwards following their defeat in battle against the armies of Saladin at Hittin in 1187. Some accounts of Christian and Arabic travellers of the 13th century mention Petra (or rather the remains left by the crusaders who stayed here), but the once mighty capital of Nabataea was destined to be completely forgotten for nearly 500 years.

Skeikh Ibrahim
Johann Ludwig Burckhardt
von Basel
gezeichnet zu Cairo im Febr. 1817.
von H. Salt Esq.

Fig. 7 – Johann Ludwig Burckhardt.

THE HISTORY OF ARCHAEOLOGICAL RESEARCH AT THE PETRA SITE

The first European to reach Petra thereafter was probably the German travel-ler, Ulrich Jasper Seetzen, who arrived as early as 1807, but did not realise the significance of the place which he had chanced upon. For this reason, the Swiss geographer and traveller, Johann Ludwig Burckhardt **(Fig. 7)**, is considered to be the first person from Western or European civilisation to rediscover the site. He visited the ruins of Petra, the lost capital of the mysterious Nabataean tribe, while assuming the name of Ibrahim ibn Abdullah, an Arab sheik. This was part of a journey he undertook between Aleppo (Syria) and Cairo, which was full of adventure. On the 22nd of August 1812, he used his cunning to gain access to the secret rock-cut city which he had heard speak of while travelling. Risking his life, the gallant traveller made notes and drew sketches in his diary, *Travels in Syria*, which subsequently appeared in print in 1822, five years after his premature death in Cairo.

News of Burckhardt's discovery of a mysterious rock-cut city spread across Europe long before the publication of his diary. As a result, three other Euro-peans dressed as Arabs managed to reach Petra in May 1818. Two of them were British naval officers (Charles Leonard Irby and James Mangles), whilst the other was an artist (William Bankes) and together they spent two days at the ruins. The next traveller to reach Petra was the Marquis Leon de Laborde, who was a Frenchman. He visited the site with the illustrator, Linant de Bellefonds, in 1826. This journey resulted in the production of 30 lithographs, which are of extraordinary value today. A few years later in 1839, David Roberts, a famous British artist, visited Petra during his journey through Egypt and the Holy Land and completed a series of sketches and drawings of the city of rock.

Systematic academic research at Petra was begun in 1896 by the Czech scholar, Alois Musil, who identified and described cult sites of the Nabataean capital, including the mysterious 'high places'. A more detailed investigation, mainly dealing with the classification of the rock façades, appeared in the first volume of the monumental work, *Die Provincia Arabia*, published between the years of 1904 and 1909 by the German academics Rudolf E. Brünnow and Alfred von Domaszewski. Over the course of two visits to Petra in 1897 and 1898, the two scholars documented and numbered over 800 rock-cut items and inscriptions and placed them on 18 detailed maps.

Gustaw Dalman was another German scholar to take an interest in the site and he visited Petra on several occasions between 1896 and 1907. His work focused mainly on religious questions concerning the Nabataean beliefs and rock-cut areas linked to cult worship, such as triclinia, votive and commemo-rative niches and stone sanctuaries.

Finally, when discussing early research in Petra, it is also worth mentioning Theodor Wiegand, Walter von Bachman and Carl Watzinger. Whilst working for the Deutsch-Türkische Denkmalschutz Kommando during the First World War, they penned descriptions of the buildings of the city centre, focusing mainly on those around Petra's main street.

Archaeological excavation work began at Petra in 1929, when George Horsfield and Agnes Conway (who would later become his wife) cleaned several tombs and houses. Further excavations were then carried out by the famous American archaeologist, William Foxwell Albright, who was the director of the American School of Oriental Research in Jerusalem at the time. In 1934, in collaboration with the Horsfields, he cleaned a site in the northern part of the city which is known today as the 'Conway Tower'. Margaret Murray and J.C. Ellis of the British School of Archaeology in Egypt later carried out archaeological work on several stone houses and tombs located in the Wadi Turkmaniyya.

After the Second World War, more precisely in 1954, excavation work began in Petra which was overseen by the Department of Antiquities of Jordan and the British School of Archaeology in Jerusalem. Over the years 1955-1956, their archaeologists cleaned the main street of the city (known as the 'Colonnaded Street') under the direction of Diana Kirkbride. In addition, they dug up several rooms belonging to shops which were located along it.

From the end of the 1950s onwards, the British archaeologist Peter Parr carried out excavations both around the entrance to the sacred precinct of the temple (known as the 'Arched Gate') and along the Colonnaded Street, where he discovered the remains of an early building from the 4th century BCE. He also investigated the southern section of the city wall as well as the Qasr al-Bint Firaun temple, in which he discovered epigraphic evidence which proved that it was dedicated to the most important Nabataean god, Dushara. Over the course of his investigations, Parr also established a chronological sequence for thin-walled ceramics which is of great worth to all Nabataean archaeologists. Aside from their chronology, he also described the development of their ceramic decoration and their typological changes.

Over the course of the 1950s and the beginning of the 1960s, a smashed column of al-Khazneh Firaun was reconstructed, some of the collapsed columns of the main street in the city centre were re-erected and the monumental gateway leading to the sacred precinct of the temple was rebuilt. All this work was carried out under the direction of George R.H. Wright.

In 1959, the American Expedition to Petra, led by Philip Hammond of the University of Utah, conducted an excavation on the terrain of al-Katuteh in cooperation with Peter Parr. The first private residence in Petra was discovered here. From 1961 to 1962, working with the Department of Antiquities of Jordan, Hammond then excavated the main theatre of Petra and from 1973 he led the work of the American Expedition to Petra in uncovering and reconstructing the so-called 'Temple of the Winged Lions'.

A little later, Fawzi Zayadine of the Department of Antiquities of Jordan collaborated with a German team of researchers from the Naturhistorisches Gesellschaft Nürnberg, led by Manfred Lindner, to investigate several tombs on the western edge of al-Khubtha. In addition, he also managed to uncover part of the interior of Qasr al-Bint Firaun. The work of the German archaeological mission under Lindner, which was conducted from 1982 to 1983, focused on the terrain of the ed-Deir plateau and the Wadi Sabra, located in the vicinity of Petra.

In the 1990s, work began on remains from the Byzantine period in Petra. During this time, a Christian basilica with excellently preserved floor mosaics was discovered, reconstructed and prepared for tourists to view. The work of the American expedition was led by Zbigniew Fiema, who today still plays an active role in uncovering the secrets of Petra as part of a Finnish expedition researching the remains of a Byzantine pilgrimage complex near Mount Aaron.

Petra is now one of the most thoroughly researched archaeological sites in the world and excavations continue to be carried out here by numerous international research expeditions. For example, researchers from the University of Basel and the Swiss-Liechtenstein Foundation for Archaeological Research Abroad (SLFA) are currently working on the residential district on the southern edge of ez-Zantur, whilst archaeologists from The Association for the Understanding of Ancient Cultures (AUAC) are active in the Wadi Farasa. Aside from the expedition working on the Temple of the Winged Lions, Americans are also researching the surroundings of the 'Great Temple' and the nearby 'Markets' area (the Joukowsky Institute for Archaeology and the Ancient World, Brown University), as well as continuing work on the "Byzantine District" (American School of Oriental Research in Amman). German researchers have meanwhile concentrated their efforts on work connected with the conservation of the façade tombs, whilst the previously mentioned Finnish expedition has begun investigating a Byzantine pilgrimage complex dating from the 5th to the 7th century situated on the broad plateau at the foot of Mount Aaron. Finally, archaeologists from Italy, under the leadership of Guido Vanini, continue to investigate remains from the time of the Crusades in the Petra area (al-Wu'eira and al-Habis).

It must also be added that there is an increasing amount of work being performed by local Jordanian archaeologists, who, under the direction of the Department of Antiquities of Jordan, are uncovering many new elements of this city of rock and putting them on display for tourists visiting Petra.

Fig. 8 – The rock-cut façade tombs in Petra.

THE FAÇADE TOMBS

The rock-cut façade tombs, undoubtedly one of Petra's biggest tourist attractions **(Fig. 8)**, have been the source of a great deal of controversy and argument between the researchers investigating them. As a result, numerous theories have been put forward over the years concerning their typology, chronology and the way in which they were created. As they constantly feature on any route taken through Petra, it is worth familiarising ourselves with their specific types.

The first person to describe and classify the façade tombs in Petra was the German scholar, Alfred von Domaszewski. In 1897, whilst journeying across Arabia with Rudolf Brünnow, he classified the façades of the rock tombs into seven main types based on their architectonic design style and the presence of classical elements.

Pylon tombs characteristically have a façade decorated in the upper section by ornamentation reminiscent of a merlon or row of crowstep **(Fig. 9)**. Depending on the number of rows of crowstep, pylon tombs are divided into two groups: tombs with only one row and those with two. Additional elements of decoration of the façade are the *torus*, cornice and flat frieze ("*fascia*" in Latin), which are included into the design in various ways. Pylon tombs from the second group can also be divided into those whose upper row of crowstep was made as a relief within the rock itself and those which had the row of crowstep built onto it. Rows of crowstep of the latter variety have often not survived to the present day.

The front walls of pylon tombs in many cases lean backwards, whilst the side walls lean inwards. This causes them to resemble the pylons of Egyptian temples and this is probably the reason why Domaszewski named the type in the way he did. Pylon tombs are the most numerous group of façade tombs in Petra.

Step tombs differ from pylon tombs in that the crowstep ornamentation is replaced by two diverging rows of steps which are

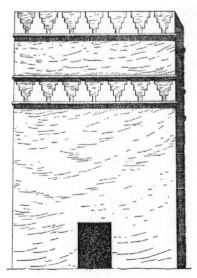

Fig. 9 – Pylon Tomb (from Brünnow, Domaszewski, Die Provincia Arabia, Fig 132).

Fig. 10 – Step Tomb (from Brünnow, Domaszewski, Die Provincia Arabia, Fig 149).

Fig. 11 – Proto-Hegr Tomb (from Brünnow, Domaszewski, Die Provincia Arabia, Fig 159).

placed in the upper part of the façade and ascend from the centre diagonally outwards (**Fig. 10**). Beneath the steps, the number of which is canonically fixed at five, a new decorative element called the *cavetto* cornice can also be found alongside the *torus* and flat frieze – *fascia*.

Proto-Hegr tombs have a similar upper façade to step tombs as they also have an attic decorated by steps ascending outwards from the centre, as well as a *cavetto* cornice, *torus* and *fascia* underneath (**Fig. 11**). The lower section of the façade decoration is formed by pilasters located to the sides which are crowned by Nabataean style capitals.

Hegr tombs owe their name to the famous ancient caravan station of central Arabia called Hegra (currently known as Mada'in Salih in Saudi Arabia), where they are the dominant rock façade type present. At first glance, they seem very similar to the proto-Hegr type, as they also have an attic with steps in the upper section and a *cavetto* cornice, *torus* and *fascia* situated underneath (**Fig. 12**). The sides of the façade likewise have pilasters crowned by Nabataean capitals. The factor that differentiates them, however, is the fact that Hegr tombs possess a classical entablature and sub-attic situated between the pilasters and upper section, whilst proto-Hegr tombs do not.

A new element incorporated into the Hegr tomb is the double frame entrance. The outer frame is formed by a classical entablature topped by a triangular gable and supported by a pair of pilasters with Nabataean capitals. The inner frame is far more variable and can take the form of either a simple, smooth frame, an architrave supported by a pair of pilasters or even a double architrave placed on pilasters topped by Nabataean capitals. On some Hegr tomb façades, the upper edge is topped by a cornice, whilst others are placed on low daises.

A variation on the Hegr form can be found in tombs whose attic floor is divided by four undersized pilasters (called dwarf pilasters) topped by Nabataean capitals (**Fig. 13**). Of these four pilasters which appear on the façade decoration, the two outer ones are aligned above angular buttresses, whilst the two inner ones are not connected to the lower part of the façade at all.

The most celebrated form of the Hegr type tomb is that of a façade decorated by two half columns located between angular pillars. The lower half of this type of façade is thus divided into three parts with the central one, located between the two half columns, containing the entrance.

Arch tombs are characterised by the fact that their top is in the form of a semicircle (or arch) which is supported by two side pillars (**Fig. 14**). It is possible to divide this type into two groups: those which have a single frame entrance and those with a double. Arch tombs are of a

Fig. 12 – Hegr Tomb (from Brünnow, Domaszewski, Die Provincia Arabia, Fig 163).

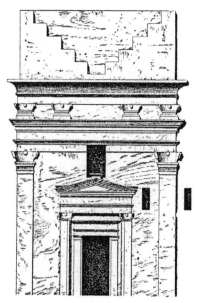

Fig. 13 – Hegr Tomb with dwarf pilasters (from Brünnow, Domaszewski, Die Provincia Arabia, Fig 169).

31

Fig. 14 – Arch Tomb (from Brünnow, Domaszewski, Die Provincia Arabia, Fig 175).

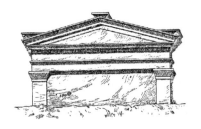

Fig. 15 – Gable Tomb (from Brünnow, Domaszewski, Die Provincia Arabia, Fig 178).

relatively small size and their height never exceeds four metres.

Gable tombs are also found in Petra. This category possesses façades which are decorated with side pilasters, topped by simple capitals, which support classical Greek entablatures **(Fig. 15)**. Architraves, flat friezes, cornices and triangular gables with consoles under the acroterion are then placed on top.

Roman Temple tombs form the final group of façade tombs at Petra. They boast the richest decoration and have the most atypical façades. The simplest form of the Roman Temple tomb is that with a façade design derived from that of the gable tombs. The decoration of these façades consists of a triangular gable resting on a classical entablature which is in turn held up by pillars **(Fig. 16)**. The pillars are formed by pilasters connected to quarter columns which are topped by Nabataean capitals. An additional element of decoration is the frame of the entrance.

According to Domaszewski, tombs belonging to the Roman Temple category include: the 'Tomb of the Roman Soldier', the 'Tomb of the Broken Pediment', the 'Obelisk Tomb' and the 'Tomb of Sextius Florentinus'. The most elaborate tombs of this category are represented by the so-called 'Royal Tombs': al-Khazneh Firaun, ed-Deir, the 'Urn Tomb', the 'Corinthian Tomb' and the 'Palace Tomb'.

Tombs of the Roman Temple type were intended for Nabataean kings, their families and the highest ranking royal officials, such as the 'royal brothers', who carried out the administration of the kingdom on behalf of the king. Thanks to an inscription found at Mada'in Salih, we also know that only members of the highest social class were able to build the richly ornamented Hegr type tombs. The slightly more modest proto-Hegr tombs were

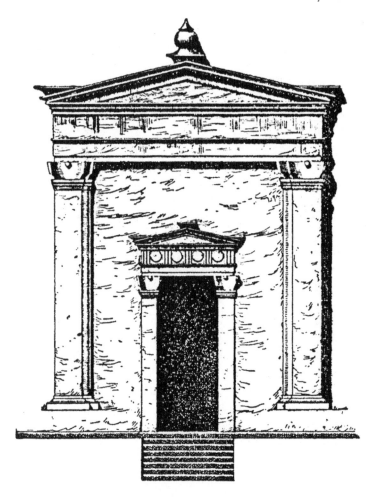

Fig. 16 – Roman Temple Tomb (from Brünnow, Domaszewski, Die Provincia Arabia, Fig 189).

built for the middle-class and also for women with the highest standing in the social hierarchy. The occupants of pylon and step tombs were mainly women and no public official was buried in either. This could mean that these types may have been designed for members of less wealthy families, a theory which is supported by the fact that they were often shared by different families. Those who could not afford to build a façade tomb, however, were placed in normal pit or shaft graves. Many of these have been discovered, especially in the Petra area.

The typological classification of the façade graves in Petra established by Domaszewski has been accepted by most researchers investigating Nabataean issues, either unreservedly or with only minor alterations. Some scholars, however, have proposed a different, somewhat simpler classification system with three main typological groups, which is also based on façade decoration. The first group of this system are the 'Assyrian' tombs, decorated by rows of crowstep, whilst the second is made up of the step tombs. The third group is that of the gable tombs and also includes all of the other façade types. The gable in question can therefore be either a regular, triangular one, an arch one or even a broken one.

Thanks to the unfinished nature of some of the rock façades in Petra, for example the 'Unfinished Tomb' at the side of al-Habis, it is possible for us to imagine how Nabataean stonemasons carried out their work.

Firstly, it would have been necessary to choose a suitable rock face and then to smoothen it until a flat, vertical surface was obtained. Only after this preparation would it have been possible to begin to cut the façade and the process would have been carried out from top to bottom. It also seems that this type of building technique did not require the use of a complex system of scaffolding to protect the craftsman at work.

Work on the rock would have been performed using a tool resembling an iron chisel at an angle of about 45 degrees to the rock face. The façades would then have been (at least partially) plastered and painted. The remnants of both stucco and paintings (in which the colours of red, yellow and blue would have dominated) still remain on several tombs. In addition, paintings discovered at Siq al-Barid (Little Petra) seem to suggest that the interiors of the tombs were also painted.

It is worth remembering that façade tombs were often just one part of a larger complex, which could also include courtyards, porticos, gardens, terraces, triclinia and water cisterns. The remains of such complexes can be found at the 'Tomb of the Roman Soldier' in the Wadi Farasa, at the 'Unaishu Tomb' on the western slope of al-Khubtha and also at the 'Turkmaniyya Tomb'.

Façade tombs were most probably built at Petra over a period of about 200 to 250 years with the first of them appearing at the turn of the 2nd and 1st centuries BCE. These would have been simple pylon tombs (with either one or two rows of crowstep) and they would have had either a cut oblong hollow above the entrance or no entrance decoration at all. Step tombs would have been built at the same time or perhaps a little later. The type of façade depended on both the financial means of its occupant and their social class.

The growing affluence of the residents of Petra resulted in the development of more elaborate façades. This could be witnessed both in the increased amount of decoration at the entrance and in the appearance of entirely new types. In the first case, the pylon and step tombs came to boast richly ornamented entrances (although the scale of this of course depended on the financial means of the owner). In the second, side pilasters and an additional attic were formed to create the proto-Hegr and Hegr types.

The driving force behind the creation of new façade types was undoubtedly the desire of the upper class to distance themselves from less wealthy members of society. In the second half of the 1st century BCE, the four tomb types previously mentioned were all being built in vastly differing decorative styles. This can be seen in the façades at Hegra which have been dated thus far. In fact, at the beginning of the 1st century CE, all types of tomb were already present here.

The most glamorous tombs of Petra, the Roman Temple tombs, also date to the beginning of the Common Era, with the vast majority of them dating to the 1st century CE. The question still remains, however, as to which precise ruler was responsible for each specific grave.

At this point, it is necessary to emphasise the fact that, aside from chronological factors, the only criteria deciding the choice of tomb to be constructed were the financial means of the owner and their position in society. The location of the tomb played no part in this decision, since in various regions of Petra hugely different types of tomb have been discovered directly next to each other.

The last precisely dated façade tomb of Petra is the Tomb of Sextius Florentinus, which dates to around 130 CE and may even have been the very last one to be built. But what could have caused the construction of tombs to cease? Above all, it was probably the fact that façade tombs were used over and over again. From an inscription discovered opposite the Obelisk Tomb, we learn that the tombs were built for many generations. This would have meant that descendants of a person who already had a tomb would not have built a new one, as they would have placed their dead in the already existing family tomb instead. Furthermore, the decreasing importance of Petra as a city and the decision to move the capital of the province to Bosra in 106 CE could have provoked a wave of migration of the upper classes towards the new seat of power, thus signalling the end of any further development of the Petraean necropolis.

Fig. 17 – Khirbet et-Tannur.

For the nomads living within its confines, the desert has always been the dwelling place of various gods, spirits and supernatural beings, some friendly to humans and others not. From the earliest times, people trying to eke out an existence in such extremely difficult conditions have sought for care, support and help from the 'ruling gods of the desert'.

The Nabataeans living in the desert areas of Arabia initially worshipped various local gods, who watched over the different types of terrain: deserts, rocks, oases and water springs. **Sa'ab** is considered to be one of these gods by certain researchers and is known from an inscription discovered at the foot of the al-Khubtha elevation as well as from other sources. According to J. T. Milik, the region of Sa'ab (which this god is supposed to have taken care of) today lies in the south-east of Kuwait, which would agree with the theory suggesting that the beginnings of Nabataean civilisation are to be sought in the region of the Persian Gulf.

Over time, as the Nabataeans began to establish permanent settlements, new gods began to appear on the scene. They were more connected to a settled rather than to a nomadic lifestyle. Gods responsible for the family hearth and home, success in business, as well as those who guarded the newly-built tombs of the 'city of the dead' therefore assumed an increasing importance. The Nabataeans also adopted some religious customs from those who lived on their territory before their rule. In this way, the Edomite god, Qaws, was added to the pantheon of their gods alongside his wife, the goddess Atargatis.

Qaws was the god of storms, lightning and life-giving rain and is therefore often compared to the Aramaic god, Hadad, and the Greek Zeus **(Fig. 18)**. One of the most important Nabataean sanctuaries was dedicated to him in Khirbet et-Tannur **(Fig. 17)** and it was here that an inscription describing Qaws as the god of Harawa (meaning 'burnt' in Arabic and possibly in reference to the nearby black basalt rock) was discovered during archaeological investigation.

Fig. 18 – The head of the statue representing the Nabataean god, Qaws. Found in Khirbet et-Tannur and now in the Archaeological Museum of Amman.

Fig. 19 – Relief with a depiction of the goddess, Atargatis. Found in Khirbet et-Tannur and now in the Archaeological Museum of Amman.

Outside Khirbet et-Tannur, however, inscriptions mentioning Qaws appear only very rarely. In the adyton of the temple, a stele was discovered presenting Qaws with a bolt of lightning in his left hand, seated on a throne with a bull and an eagle standing either side of him. His wife, **Atargatis**, the goddess of the harvest and agricultural fertility, was seated beside him. Her importance in the pantheon of Nabataean gods rose steeply under the rule of Rabbel II, when agriculture became the main source of income for the majority of Nabataeans. It was therefore mainly her images which adorned the temple of Khirbet et-Tannur **(Fig. 19)**, which was further developed both under the rule of Rabbel II and also after Nabataea's annexation by the Romans. Atargatis is often presented in the company of lions and eagles. An inscription describing her as the patron goddess of the town of Hierapolis (on the Euphrates in northern Syria) has also been discovered next to a rock-cut idol with schematically marked eyes in Petra.

Great changes in the religious customs of the Nabataeans occurred as the result of trade and cultural links with the Romano-Hellenic world. This caused their own gods to be compared and identified with those of Greece, Rome and Egypt.

The most important Nabataean god was **Dushara** (in Greek "*Dusares*"), which means the 'Lord of Sharah' in Arabic ("*Du-as-Shara*") **(Fig. 20)**.

Dushara was at first a local god watching over the mountainous region of as-Shara. Later, when Petra became the capital of the

Fig. 20 – Bas-relief depicting the Nabataean god, Dushara. Now in the Archaeological Museum of Damascus.

Nabataean state, Dushara rose to the rank of the most important deity of the local pantheon and his status was not to be diminished by the later Roman annexation of *Arabia Petraea*. Tertullian, a Christian theologian living at the turn of the 2nd and 3rd centuries CE stated that: "*Every province and city has its own god: Syria has Astarte, whilst Arabia has Dusares*". In this same period, a festival known as the *Actia Dusaria* took place every four years in Bosra. According to the anonymous author of a lexicon known as the *Liber Suda* (which appeared at the end of the 10th century CE, but made use of much earlier sources), Dushara was presented as a regular, rectangular stone (or 'betyl'), which was high on four feet but broad on two and stood on a base of pure gold. During ritual sacrifices at the temple, a libation was offered by pouring the blood of the victim onto the betyl stone. This description is confirmed by images of Dushara's temple on Roman coins from Bosra, which is symbolised by a rectangular betyl.

Dushara was seen to be the creator of the world, the lord of the sun, the earth and the harvest. Several inscriptions name him 'the god of our Lord' or 'the god of Rabbel'. This supports the theory that Dushara was also the protector of the royal family. An inscription found in Oboda in the Negev also describes him as the god of an area called Gaia, which is located in the vicinity of Petra, more precisely where the village of Wadi Musa now stands.

Over time, Dushara started to be connected to Zeus and Dionysus. In Miletus (in modern day Turkey), a carved inscription was found from the 1ˢᵗ century BCE which was dedicated by Syllaeus to the honour of Zeus-Dusares. The Byzantine author, Hesychius, however, when writing in the 5ᵗʰ century CE, stated that *"Dusares is the Nabataean Dionysus"*. In Petra, it is possible to see a very interesting stone relief which is found on the processional way from the Wadi Farasa to the peak of Zibb Atuf, which has been identified by some researchers as the image of Dushara-Dionysus. According to another hypothesis, it is not Dushara but the Nabataean god, **A'ra**, who should be equated to the Greek god Dionysus. A'ra was the god of fertility and vegetation, and incense was burned in his honour on oblong altars. He was also a patron god of Bosra, which is attested by several inscriptions from this city. In later times, he started to be identified with Dushara, perhaps because of the shifting of the capital to Bosra, and it could be that in this period Dushara-A'ra started to be linked to Dionysus.

Dushara also occupied top position in the Nabataean trinity, a group of three deities. For most people of the Ancient East, the trinity comprised a father god, mother god and their child, who was most commonly depicted as a young man. In the Nabataean pantheon, however, Dushara was joined by two females, Allat and al-Uzza.

The goddess **Allat** is considered to have been the wife or mother of Dushara in the Nabataean pantheon **(Fig. 21)**. Her name is a shortened form of the Arabic expression "al-Illahat", which simply means 'goddess'. Judging by the number of inscriptions dedicated to her that have been discovered thus far, it is clear that she was the most worshipped goddess across all of Arabia and southern Syria. She was considered the patron of travellers, animal drivers and warriors. Herodotus described 'Allat' (referring to her as Alilat) as an Arabic name for Aphrodite. Many later writers connected her with Urania or Athena, since she was often given the attributes of the Greek goddess of

Fig. 21 – Relief depicting the goddess, Allat. Now in the Archaeological Museum of Damascus.

war and soldiers prayed to her to grant them success in battle. We do not yet know of any inscriptions mentioning Allat from Petra, but a relief present-ing Athena within the sacred precinct of the temple of Qasr al-Bint Firaun suggests that she could have been worshipped here, perhaps in one of the side adytons.

An important site of the goddess Allat was a temple constructed in Wadi Ramm, on the path between Petra and Hegra, which was a rest area for all the merchants and their caravans travelling along it. From an inscription found nearby, it seems that she was also a patron god of Bosra. This is not surprising, considering the fact that in another text she is described as the "*mother of the gods of our Lord Rabbel*", the monarch who moved the capital from Petra to Bosra.

Al-Uzza, meaning 'almighty', was the other female god of the Nabataean trinity. Her cult was practised all over Nabataea and also beyond its borders. This goddess was often equated to Aphrodite with one example coming from a bilingual inscription from 9 BCE discovered on the Greek island of Kos. On many inscriptions she is mentioned alongside another god, most commonly Dushara. In Petra, just next to the processional way to the summit of al-Khubtha, an empty niche can be found, next to which is the inscription: "*This is the stele of al-Uzza and the Lord of the Home (Dushara?)…*". In the vicinity of Ayn esh-Shalaleh in Wadi Ramm, two betyls of Al-Uzza have also been discovered, one alongside an image of the god, al-Kutba (see below), and the other, as was the case in Petra, with the Lord of the Home, most probably Dushara. The inscription on the latter reads: "*This is al-Uzza and the Lord of the Home….*". Betyls identified as images of al-Uzza often possess stylised eyes and noses, sometimes in the form of a star. The most beautiful example of this comes from the Temple of the Winged Lions in Petra, which would confirm the suspicion that this temple was dedicated to al-Uzza-Aphrodite.

The great goddess of the world of the dead was **Manat**, which means 'bad fortune'. The Nabataeans worshipped her as the tender and protector of tombs and also as guarantor that their last will and testament would be carried out correctly. Manat was often identified with the Greek goddesses Tyche (the equivalent of the Roman Fortuna) and Nemesis (the goddess of revenge). Her attribute is supposed to have been the length measurement of a cubit, which symbolised fate. This goddess was mainly worshipped in southern Nabataea; the name Manat (written as Manawat), for example, appears on tomb inscriptions eight times in Hegra (Mada'in Salih). We do not, however, know of any inscriptions from Petra bearing her name.

The Arab historian Hisham ibn al-Kalabi, who lived from 747 to 819, wrote in his work "Kitab al-Asnam" ('Book of Gods') that Allat, al-Uzza and Manat together formed a trinity of goddesses worshipped in Arabia before the appearance of Mohammed and his monotheistic religion. According to ibn al-Kalabi, Arab pilgrims cried out to "*Allat, al-Uzza and Manat, dignified blue ladies, who we ask to intercede for us*" while processing around the al-Ka'aba sanctuary in Mecca. The Qur'an also mentions that Arabs worshipped this trinity of goddesses in pre-Islamic times. According to the holy book of Islam, Allat, al-Uzza and Manat were said to be the daughters of Allah himself.

Shay al-Qaum, the 'Protector of the Tribe', was another of the gods worshipped by the Nabataeans. He was the companion god who looked after and protected those wandering through the desert. As the consumption of wine was strictly forbidden within his cult, he was seen as the opponent and rival of the Greek god, Dionysus, and was connected more to the nomadic rather than to the settled traditions of the Nabataeans. His cult developed greatly in the 1st century CE as a reaction to the increasing number of people following Dionysus. It can thus be seen that prohibition of wine consumption and alcohol in general existed in Arabia long before Islam appeared on the scene, a fact about which Diodurus Siculus also wrote. Shay al-Qaum does not seem to have been particularly popular in Petra, as no inscriptions dedicated to him have yet been found there.

Al-Kutba was the patron of literature, trade and travel, which is why he is often associated with the Greek Hermes and Roman Mercury. In the previously mentioned Wadi Ramm, close to the Ayn esh-Shalaleh spring, a betyl of al-Kutba with eyes in the form of a star stands in a rectangular niche directly next to another niche containing a betyl of the goddess al-Uzza. The inscription underneath announces: "*Al-Kutba, who is in Gaia*", a place located near Petra. In Petra itself, his name only appears twice, one of them being on the way to the region of al-Madras, which was dedicated to Dushara.

One of the most popular foreign gods who were worshipped at

Fig. 22 – Terracotta figurine representing the goddess Isis. Found in Petra. Now in the Archaeological Museum of Amman.

Petra was the Egyptian goddess, **Isis (Fig. 22)**, the wife of Osiris. Her cult spread dramatically in the Hellenistic and Roman periods across both Egypt and Arabia, which it reached thanks to trade links between the two regions and the activity of Alexandrian artisans in Petra. The symbol of Isis, a sun shield covered by horns and spikes, adorns the central acroterion gable of al-Khazneh Firaun. Two small votive niches were also dedicated to her in the Wadi ad-Dalaw and at the entrance to the Wadi as-Siyyagh. In both cases, she is presented sitting on a throne. In addition, several terracotta figures of the Egyptian goddess have been discovered over the course of Petraean excavation work.

Fig. 23 – Donkey – a convenient way to explore Petra.

PRACTICAL INFORMATION

The Petra Visitor Centre is located at the entrance to Petra and is thus the starting point of every visit. This enormous complex consists of hotel and restaurant sectors, tourist service areas and a vast car park for both buses and private cars. The Petra Visitor Centre is also the place to buy tickets to enter the Petra archaeological site and the place where you can gain all the information you require for your visit, hire the services of a guide and obtain a means of transport **(Fig. 23)**. Additionally, there are many souvenir and food and drink shops, a small bookshop and a place where you can exchange currency.

Opening Hours

The archaeological site of Petra and the Petra Visitor Centre are open every day from 6am to 6pm in the summer months and from 6am to 4pm in the winter months.

Tickets

Tickets to Petra are sold at the entrance to the Petra Visitor Centre. The price of tickets varies according to the length of your planned visit to the site and the length of your stay in Jordan.

1. Ticket prices for visitors spending at least one night in Jordan:
   One day pass: 50 JD
   Two day pass: 55 JD
   Three day pass: 60 JD
2. Ticket prices for visitors not spending a night in Jordan (e.g. on a one day excursion from Sinai or Israel):
   One day pass: 90 JD

Be aware that tickets can only be bought in cash in Jordanian dinars (JD). Credit cards are not yet accepted.

Maps and Tourist Brochures

Free maps and brochures about Petra are available at the entrance to the Petra Visitor Centre in English, French, German, Spanish, Italian and Arabic. More detailed maps and guides can be bought in the shops on the premises of the centre, including the small bookshop. We recommend the detailed *Tourist Map of Petra* (scale 1/5000) issued by the Royal Jordanian Geographic Centre.

Guides

The services of a licensed guide can be acquired in the Petra Visitor Centre, although this is mainly of use to those wishing to visit areas away from the central part of Petra. The centre offers guides who speak English, French, Italian and Arabic.

Getting There, Accommodation and Other Useful Information

Petra lies in southern Jordan near the village of Wadi Musa. It is very straightforward to travel here from Amman (which can be reached by plane from every corner of the world) or Aqaba (which has a land border with Israel and receives ships from Egypt) with a hired car (around 25-30 JD per day) or on local transport (bus, minibus). Information on this topic can be found on the website *visitjordan.com*. In Wadi Musa, there are a whole host of hotels for people of all different budgets, ranging from the cheap tourist hotels such as An-Anabat (which has 3 different branches) to the 5-star Mövenpick Resort, which stands at the very entrance to ancient Petra. Reservations can be made online through services such as *tripadvisor.com, booking.com* or *trivago.com*. A great deal of valuable information on Petra itself can also be found on the pages *visitpetra.jo* and *petranationaltrust.org*.

Suggested Itineraries

Petra itself could be visited for weeks on end. Most people, however, have only one day, or perhaps two or three, in which to see the site. For this reason, this guide includes descriptions of the most popular tourist trails, alongside those which are less well-known **(Fig. 24)**. For all routes, the level of difficulty has been stated as well as the predicted time required to complete it. This should allow you to tailor your route to suit both your timeframe and physical condition.

One Day

With only one day to see Petra, Trail 1 (The Siq – The Pharaoh's Treasury – The Theatre) and Trail 2 (The City Centre (South): The Colonnaded Street – The Great Temple – The Qasr al-Bint Firaun Temple) are your best bet to begin the day. Then, after a short break to visit the museums in the centre of Petra and a possible rest (including lunch) in the small tourist centre, Trail 3 (The Wadi ed-Deir – The Monastery) can be followed, before returning from the centre of Petra on Trail 4 (The City Centre (North): The Temple of the Winged Lions – The Petra Church – The Royal Tombs).

Fig. 24 – Map of Petra with the locations of the most important monuments and trails described in the guide.

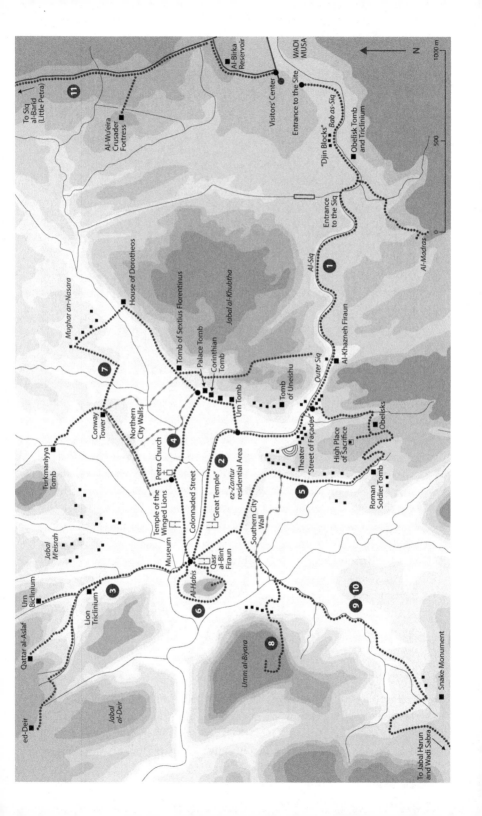

Fig. 25 – Hegr Tomb in the tourist centre.

Two Days

With two full days to see Petra, the first could be spent in the manner suggested above for a one day visit. The second could then begin with Trail 5 (The High Place of Sacrifice – The Wadi Farasa – Ez-Zantur) and after a short break continue with Trail 6 (Al-Habis – The Acropolis) and Trail 7 (North Petra: Conway Tower – Mughar an-Nasara – Al-Khubtha).

It often turns out that those visiting Petra only have one-and-a-half days in which to see the site. In such a situation, it is advisable to do Trail 1 (The Siq – The Pharaoh's Treasury – The Theatre), Trail 2 (The City Centre (South): The Colonnaded Street – The Great Temple – The Qasr al-Bint Firaun Temple) and Trail 4 (The City Centre (North): The Temple of the Winged Lions – The Petra Church – The Royal Tombs) on the first day. The second day would then follow Trail 5 (The High Place of Sacrifice – The Wadi Farasa – Ez-Zantur) and Trail 3 (The Wadi ed-Deir – The Monastery).

Three Days

Tourists with three days to visit Petra should follow the same routes as in the two day programme on the first two days. The third day can then be spent on a longer excursion (Trails 8-10), the most interesting of which from a sightseeing point of view is undoubtedly the trip to Mount Aaron (Trail 9).

Fig. 26 – Reservoir al-Birka.

Visiting the Rock-Cut City

The current starting point of a visit to Petra is the recently built tourist centre in the town of Wadi Musa, the facilities of which include a hotel, restaurant, massive car park, tourist service points and a great many souvenir shops. It also provides an authentic titbit of what is to come in the form of a rock-cut Nabataean façade tomb situated in the restaurant **(Fig. 25)**. This is a Hegr type tomb, which is additionally fronted by a courtyard and flanked on both sides by portico columns, also rock-cut.

Before entering the archaeological park itself, it is possible to view the remains of an interesting Nabataean building, although it is naturally not as visually impressive as the centre of Petra itself. It is also worth noting the two enormous stone reservoirs, named al-Birka **(Fig. 26)**, which collected the precious water flowing from Moses' Well. The southern reservoir has preserved itself better than the northern and measures 18 by 32 metres. It was able to hold 2,500 cubic metres of water, which was then transported via terracotta channels to the city centre. The remains of five pottery kilns are located in the vicinity (currently not on display to the public), in which vessels would have been made in both Nabataean times as well as in the later Roman and Byzantine periods.

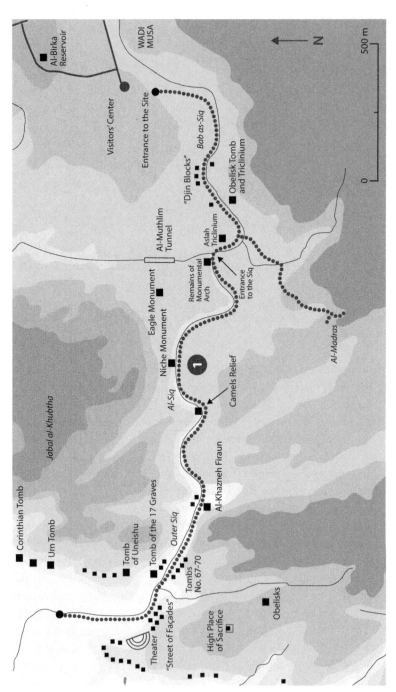

Al-Birka
Reservoir

WADI
MUSA

Visitors' Center

Entrance to the Site

Bab as-Siq

"Djin Blocks"

Obelisk Tomb
and Triclinium

Al-Muthlim
Tunnel

Aslah
Triclinium

Remains of
Monumental
Arch

Entrance
to the Siq

Eagle Monument

Niche Monument

Al-Siq

Al-Madras

Camels Relief

Jabal al-Khubtha

Corinthian Tomb

Um Tomb

Tomb
of Uneishu

Tomb of the 17 Graves

Outer Siq

Al-Khazneh Firaun

"Street of Façades"

Theater

Tombs
No. 67-70

High Place
of Sacrifice

Obelisks

N

500 m

0

Fig. 27 – Trail No. 1.

The Siq – The Pharaoh's Treasury – The Theatre (Fig. 27)

This is undoubtedly the must-do trail for all those visiting Petra. It does not require much physical effort as it contains no lengthy or steep climbs. Walking along the gorge, the trail includes many highlights, such as the Obelisk Tomb, the famous al-Khazneh Firaun, the Theatre and dozens of the rock-cut tombs which have made Petra's name. The time required (to go there and back) is approximately two to three hours depending on your physical condition, the time of day and ... your level of interest in the individual monuments.

The area you enter after leaving the tourist centre of Wadi Musa, which leads to the centre of Petra along an incredible rock gorge, is known as as-Siq (meaning 'gorge' or 'canyon') to the locals, whilst the twisting, tapering valley at the beginning of it is named Bab as-Siq, ('gorge gateway' in Arabic) **(Fig. 28)**. Just after entering the valley, where there are currently two main paths demarcated (one for tourists on foot and the other for those riding horses, donkeys or camels (dromedary camels with one hump to be precise)), it is possible to see the first examples of Nabataean façade tombs. Located within the so-called south-eastern necropolis of Petra, these are, however, fairly modest façades, which mostly appear on step or proto-Hegr tombs.

Fig. 28 – Bab as-Siq Valley. View from the Obelisk Tomb.

A moment later, you will come across a few freestanding figures to your right in the form of three regularly shaped stone blocks with the appearance of towers. Just in front of these, on a small rock to the left (which is a de facto tomb), it is possible to see the well-preserved bas-relief of an obelisk standing on a rectangular podium **(Fig. 29)**. This obelisk is an example of a *nefesh* (a Semitic word meaning 'person' or 'soul'), which is a symbolic representation of the souls of the dead who would have been buried inside the tomb upon which it was carved.

Fig. 29 – Tomb with an engraved obelisk.

The towers mentioned above are called *Sahrij* in Arabic, meaning water tank, or *Djin*, meaning ghost **(Fig. 30)**. In all of Petra, archaeologists have so far identified 20 structures of this type. Scholars do not, however, agree as to whether they should be treated as monumental betyls (symbols of the Nabataean god Dushara) or as altars which were dedicated to him. They may, however, have simply been regular tombs. Taking into account the results of archaeological research carried out thus far, it seems that this latter theory is probably correct, as funerary chambers have been discovered in some, whilst in others traces of decorations reminiscent of typical Nabataean tomb facades have been found. Further evidence of the final theory is provided by the three Djin blocks themselves: the first bears traces of a crowstep frieze (typical of Nabataean façade tombs); the central one, although bereft of decoration, clearly includes an entrance to a funerary chamber; the last (and biggest), is decorated by half columns, pilasters and batten levels and

Fig. 30 – Djin Blocks.

possesses a deep niche at the top (not visible from below) which was probably where the deceased was once placed.

Behind the last Djin block, to the right-hand (northern) side, is the
entrance to a small valley, which contains some beautifully preserved Hegr
type tomb façades.

About fifty metres further along, on the other side of the Wadi Musa, it is
possible to visit both the most interesting and the largest building in Bab as-
Siq, the joint structure of the Obelisk Tomb and the Bab as-Siq Triclinium,
which is cut out of yellow sandstone **(Fig. 31)**.

The relatively simple tomb façade is formed by four stone obelisks, approximately seven metres in height, standing on rectangular bases. The entrance
to the tomb is located between the central obelisks, above which a small
niche containing the badly-preserved figure of a man standing in a toga can
be seen. Some researchers claim that both this figure and the four flanking
obelisks symbolise the souls of the dead who would have been placed in the
five niches within the funerary chamber itself. These obelisks would thus be
monumental *nefashot*.

The entrance to the tomb is decorated by two pilasters supporting a classical entablature bearing a triglyph-metope frieze. The remains of a small
courtyard with an altar reminiscent of the type found in Nabataean high
places and a pit grave cut into the centre of it can be seen in front. The
interior consists of a single funerary chamber with the five aforementioned
niches cut into the side and back walls. The most interesting of these is a

Fig. 31 – Obelisk Tomb and Bab as-Siq Triclinium.

niche of the *arcosolium* type, which is cut into the back wall and decorated by pilasters supporting a semicircular gable.

The Obelisk Tomb is unique among the rock sites of Petra. It is reminiscent of Egyptian monuments and the design of the façade calls to mind the famous temple of Pharaoh Ramses II in Abu Simbel (Egypt). In this case, however, the mighty figure of Ramses is replaced by obelisks, which according to Nabataean tradition symbolised the dead residing in the tomb. It is also worth noting the unusual mix of Egyptian elements (obelisks) with classical motives (e.g. pilasters, a frieze and a male figure), which makes the Obelisk Tomb one of the most eclectic examples of Nabataean architecture. Researchers have, however, experienced some difficulty in establishing its dating. It is probably one of the earliest façades of Petra (1st century BCE), but it is also possible that the last person to be laid to rest here, undoubtedly symbolised by the man in the toga, was placed here much later (1st century CE). This theory is supported by the distinctive niche (*arcosolium*) in the back wall, which is in a decorative style suggesting the second half of the 1st century CE.

The usage of the Obelisk Tomb in a later period can also be attested by the building known as the Bab as-Siq Triclinium, which is found below and slightly to the right of its façade. In Latin, the word *triclinium* signifies a feasting hall with benches situated along three of its walls. The Nabataeans, however, used certain triclinia, as well as the somewhat smaller biclinia (in which benches were placed on only two sides of the room), to consume ritual meals honouring their dead. Meals were therefore probably taken in the Bab as-Siq Triclinium as part of the funerary ceremonies for those who were laid to rest here in the later part of the Obelisk Tomb's use. It is worth looking inside the construction to see the remains of the stone benches ("*klinae*" in Greek) which were once feasted on to honour the dead. The Triclinium façade, although badly damaged by the hand of time, still possesses clear traits of fully developed late Nabataean architecture. Architectonic elements, such as gables (broken and arch) and pilasters, topped by Nabataean capitals (both regular and undersized), allow us to date the construction of this stylistically intriguing building to the 1st century CE.

Directly opposite the Obelisk Tomb and the Bab as-Siq Triclinium, on the other side of the valley, a rock-cut Nabataean-Greek bilingual Inscription **(Fig. 32)** is carved five metres above the ground. It informs us that a certain Abdomanchos, son of Achaios, built a tomb here for both himself and his children during the reign of King Malichus. Some researchers believe (despite a lack of direct evidence) that this inscription refers to the Obelisk Tomb, which would therefore have been built under a king by the name of

Fig. 32 – The bilingual inscription.

Malichus. The problematic aspect of this is the fact that two different kings had this name, although the character and style of the inscription suggest that Malichus I (58-30 BCE) is the more likely candidate. This would also agree with the suggested dating of the creation of the Obelisk Tomb. On the other hand, however, taking into account the dating of the Triclinium and the possible placing of a fifth deceased person within the Obelisk Tomb, the inscription could perhaps also come from the reign of King Malichus II (40-70 CE).

Close to the Obelisk Tomb, a small path bears off to the left of the main road to central Petra. This leads through a passage cut into the rock (which can be covered in fifteen minutes) to the suburb of al-Madras **(Fig. 33)**. One of the Nabataean high places is located here, as well as numerous rock-cut cisterns, niches, steps and rooms. High places were cult places typical of the Nabataeans which normally consisted of rock-cut courtyards, ritual water basins, stone benches and altars. An inscription discovered nearby informs

Fig. 33 – Rock-cut cistern in the area of al-Madras.

us that the region of al-Madras was dedicated to the Nabataean god, Dushara. The whole area, which is wild and seldom visited by tourists, is also worth a detour for its fantastic lunar landscape. From the al-Madras area it is possible to cross the vast plateau of Zarnuk al-Hureimiye to the Wadi al-Jarra (the 'Valley of the Urn'), which leads down towards the Siq and joins it precisely where al-Khazneh Firaun proudly stands.

Standing at the entrance to the Obelisk Tomb, it is also possible to make out a narrow path on the other side of the valley which leads along it before

Fig. 34 – Aslah Triclinium Complex.

reaching the group of buildings known as the Aslah Triclinium Complex
(Fig. 34). Apart from the triclinium itself, the complex also contains a broad
funerary chamber, numerous rock-cut pit graves and votive niches, as well
as a cistern with its accompanying channels hollowed out of the rock. The
complex is located directly above the entrance to the Siq and forms part of
the north-eastern necropolis of Petra, which stretches across both sides of
Bab as-Siq. Above all, the triclinium is worthy of inspection for the well-
preserved Nabataean inscription on its back wall, which mentions a man
by the name of Aslah, who erected the whole complex in honour of the
god Dushara in the first year of King Obodas' rule, the son of King Aretas.
This inscription is dated by most researchers to 96/95 BCE. Thanks to this,
the Aslah Triclinium represents the oldest building discovered thus far in
Petra which has a confirmed date of creation. On the same wall, much later
Bedouin carvings of dromedary camels, horses and even planes can be seen.
An eagle-eyed observer will also be able to discern other Nabataean carvings,
an *aedicule* and a betyl symbolising Dushara.

The Bab as-Siq valley ends in a barrier construction, known as 'The
Dam', which was built in 1964. It is located at a site which originally contained a Nabataean dam, built in the 1st century CE, to protect the Siq
from the large amount of water flowing down from the mountains during the rainy season **(Fig. 35)**. The excess water was directed to a massive
tunnel nearly 90 metres in length which was cut into the rock nearby (the
al-Muthlim Tunnel). From here the water journeyed via channels across

Fig. 35 – The Dam, the Tunnel and the Djin Block at the entrance to the Siq.

the Wadi Muthlim, the Wadi Mataha and then around the al-Khubtha elevation, before finally reaching the centre of Petra. This path can still be covered on foot today, but it must be remembered that it is a much harder journey than that through the Siq, as it requires the scaling of rock walls up to two metres in height.

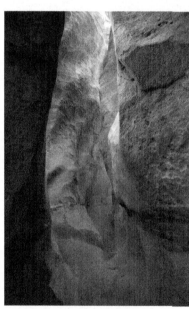

The reward for your efforts is the pleasure of wandering through a fascinating rock gorge (sometimes referred to as 'Little Siq'), which at its narrowest point is less than one metre in breadth **(Fig. 36)**. Be warned! This route is off limits in the winter and spring (the rainy season) due to the risk of drowning in the event of the gorge rapidly filling with water. No escape route exists!

Rock-cut bas-reliefs of funerary stelae (now invisible), which were similar in style to the ones opposite the Djin blocks, once featured on the rock wall opposite the dam. One of these was of particular

Fig. 36 – The 'Little Siq'.

Fig. 37 – The Eagle Monument.

interest since it bore the Semitic name of Petra, "*Reqem*". Just above the entrance to the tunnel, a further Djin block can be seen. It is decorated by a row of crowstep frieze and has an entrance to a funerary chamber visible from ground level. A path runs next to this, which leads above the tunnel to The Eagle Monument **(Fig. 37)**, a rock-cut relief presenting a standing eagle. This is situated in a niche flanked by two pilasters, which are topped by smooth capitals.

Beyond the dam mentioned above, the Siq begins. Over a kilometre in length, it wends its way through a rock canyon and is the main entrance to Petra from the east **(Fig. 38)**. Ancient travellers would have taken this route from both the so-called Kings' Highway and the Roman-built *Via Nova Traiana*. At first, the Siq does not seem particularly impressive, as its walls only reach about a dozen metres in height. Go a bit further, however, and you will soon be able to admire

Fig. 38 – The Siq.

Fig. 39 – The remains of the Arch at the entrance to the Siq.

rocks which seem to reach as high as the sky.

Just before entering the gorge, one can observe the remains of a monumental arch built at the beginning of the 2nd century CE to both sides. It would once have risen 20 metres above the level of the paved path which led to the centre **(Fig. 39)**. The first travellers to reach Petra in the 19th century would still have been able to admire its beauty, but it was unfortunately destroyed around 1896, probably as the result of an earthquake. Niches flanked by pilasters have, however, survived to the present day and it can be seen that an additional arch had started to be built above them. The remains of this can be seen to the south of the entrance.

Across the whole length of the rock gorge, channels cut into the rock are also visible on both sides. These channels would have formed part of the waterworks system which supplied the centre of Petra with water from Moses' Well. Terracotta pipes were placed into these channels and their ends connected and plugged by a special kind of mortar. This would all have then been covered by stone slabs, some of which can still be seen in several places within the canyon.

In both Nabataean and Roman times, the Siq was laid with large, flat blocks of hard sandstone to create a paved road, fragments of which remain today in many places. On the walls of the canyon, it is possible to see around a dozen commemorative and votive niches sculpted out of the rock, which bear depictions of the Nabataean gods in the form of rectangular betyls. One of the first and most interesting is a votive niche with an obelisk (barely visible today) standing between two pilasters. These support a classical entablature with a triangular gable, above which stand six small betyls symbolising gods **(Fig. 40)**. A well-trained eye, using a little imagination, should be able to pick out heavily eroded garlands and even…an Egyptian sun disc with outstretched wings.

Of equal interest is the Niche Monument, which is cut out of a freestanding rock about halfway through the gorge **(Fig. 41)**. This nearly two-and-a-

Fig. 40 – Votive niche with an obelisk on the rock face of the Siq.

half metre high recess is framed by pilasters supporting a classical entablature with a Doric frieze. The two betyls inside it are schematic representations of gods, most probably Dushara and al-Uzza. The larger god possesses schematically marked eyes and a nose. Archaeologists believe that the niche was cut in the 1st century CE, probably during the reign of Malichus II.

A broad niche containing ten steles placed in a row is also worth taking a moment to observe (it is visible to the right (northern) side, at a height of

Fig. 41 – The Niche Monument.

Fig. 42 – Niche with 10 betyls on the rock face of the Siq.

about four metres); the largest betyl in the centre is accompanied by three medium size images to the right and by six small ones to the left **(Fig. 42)**.

A little further along, one can notice a whole series of niches to the left, amongst which two stand out. One contains a hemispherical betyl (omphalos?), whilst the other contains the figure of a goddess (perhaps al-Uzza) flanked by two lions or leopards **(Fig. 43)**. Below this second niche, an

Fig. 43 – Rock wall with carved niches within the Siq.

inscription is visible bearing the name of a certain Sabinus, son of Alexandros, who must have been a Greek merchant dwelling in Petra.

An exceptional sight appears about a dozen metres further on. It takes the form of a massive stone relief presenting a figure, undoubtedly a merchant, who is leading three dromedary camels in the direction of the city centre (**Fig. 44**). Although only the legs of the merchant and camels seem to have remained intact, a closer inspection reveals the bodies of the animals. A second display of this type lies a little further along the way to the centre of Petra, but this one only features two camels. It is true that both reliefs are currently in a very badly-preserved state, but they nevertheless may help one to imagine the canyon in all its former glory. In its heyday, it would have been richly decorated with bas-reliefs, niches, depictions of gods and perhaps also ornamented paintings. Yet all of this was to be wiped out by the annual spring floods, which, after the destruction of the dam that protected the entrance, propelled a mass of water, earth and stones through the Siq, obliterating the decoration of its walls in the process.

Fig. 44 – Rock relief of a merchant leading three camels.

Continuing further along the canyon, you will pass more remains of paving stones and aqueducts running down both sides. Then, at a certain point, when the canyon again abruptly narrows and the rocks seem to be closing in over you, you will stop dead in your tracks as your eyes feast on the most breathtaking sight (**Fig. 45**). In front of you lies the most beautiful building of Petra, Jordan and perhaps the entire Near East: the Pharaoh's Treasury

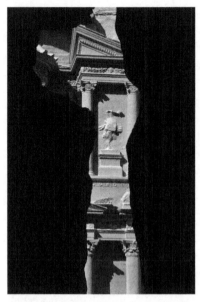

Fig. 45 – Façade of the Pharaoh's Treasury emerging from behind the rocks of the Siq.

(in Arabic known as "al-Khazneh Firaun") **(Fig. 46)**. It should come as no surprise that it is extremely difficult to contemplate this monument on your own today. Indeed, at all hours of the day, hordes of tourists congregate here to admire this miracle of ancient architecture. The rock façade of the Treasury takes on different hues depending on the time at which you view it. In the morning, lit up by the rays of the rising sun, it has a yellowish appearance. This gradually turns to orange, before beige and light bronze come to dominate in the afternoon. Finally, via a delicate pink, it turns an expressive red before sunset.

In 1911, the German scholar, Gustaw Dalman, described the front of the Treasury as *"an improbably perfectly constructed façade, belonging to the most beautiful ancient buildings of the Near East still standing in modern times"*. He was right. Travelling the world today, it is possible to visit many marvellous sites containing ancient architecture (from the Mayan pyramids of Mexico to the Roman Colosseum and the temple of Borobudur in Java), but it is extremely rare to see artistic brilliance and perfect execution combined in such an extraordinary and picturesque location. It is even rarer that such a monument has survived to our times in such excellent condition. Apart from the lower section, which was partly destroyed by swollen waters flowing from the Wadi Musa in the rainy season, the Pharaoh's Treasury has only suffered at the hands of iconoclasts (Byzantine, Arab and maybe even Nabataean), who tried to efface the figural presentation of its decoration.

The architect who created this work (and probably also chose its precise location) was for certain a great aesthete, if not a genius. However, it could be true that it is only from a modern day perspective that the Pharaoh's Treasury appears so fantastic and unreal. For the Nabataeans, at least initially, it may have been seen as an utterly foreign element which had invaded their city space. Only with time, as the process of Hellenisation and then Romanisation altered their aesthetic outlook, would they have been able to fully appreciate its artistic value. In any case, it is precisely thanks to this building that

Petra appeared on a very recently published list of the Seven Wonders of the Ancient World alongside such stunning architectural achievements as the Roman Colosseum, the Incan Machu Picchu and the Great Wall of China.

Cut out of reddish-pink sandstone, the façade of the Treasury is 38.77 metres high, 24.9 metres wide and is formed of two floors. The lower storey calls to mind a Hellenistic temple with its six mighty columns (the central

Fig. 46 – Al-Khazneh Firaun – The Pharaoh's Treasury.

two of which are freestanding), topped by Corinthian capitals, which support a sophistically ornamented entablature. Its decoration consists of cups flanked by sphinxes which alternate with vegetal ornamentation.

Above the four central columns, a richly decorated triangular gable rises, which is in turn topped by an attic supporting the upper floor. A bust of the god or ruler to whom the building was dedicated most probably once adorned the central part of the tympanum, although other theories suggest it was perhaps the figure of an eagle or the head of Medusa/Gorgon. The latter would have had an apotropaic (guarding against evil powers) significance. An interesting decorative element of the gable is found in the central acroterion, upon which an observant eye can discern the motive of a cow horn amongst the vegetal motives, a symbol of the Egyptian goddess, Isis. The side acroterions of the gable, which take the form of palmettes, have preserved themselves extraordinarily well. This is in stark contrast to the dire condition of the outer acroterion of the lower floor, which probably once bore sphinxes or lions. Rider figures on the bas-relief located between the side half columns are in similarly poor condition. They represent the divine twin brothers, the "Dioscuri", who were the sons of Zeus and the Spartan queen, Leda.

The upper floor of the Treasury façade **(Fig. 47)** bears an extremely well-executed depiction of a tholos (a small, circular building), surrounded by a double colonnade. Between the columns of the bas-relief (both the outer ones and those of the tholos itself), one can discern figures standing on plinths. In this way, the artist wanted to show us that there were statues of gods and mythical creatures between the columns of the building (which itself was a prototype of the Treasury). It is difficult to decipher who exactly is shown on this relief today, but the central figure on the tholos is most probably the goddess Tyche/Fortuna, which is indicated by the cornucopia which she holds. Other researchers, however, believe her to be the Egyptian goddess, Isis, who equates to the Nabataean al-Uzza. At the rear, on the sides of the tholos, images of the goddess of victory, Nike/Victoria, are sculpted. The most mysterious figures are those on the relief underneath the broken gables. As they seem to be dressed in short skirts and are wielding something resembling axes above their heads, they are considered to be dancing Amazonian warrior women.

The central part of the tholos is topped by a conical roof, on top of which is a single Corinthian capital bearing a nearly four-metre-high stone urn **(Fig. 48)**. According to Bedouin legend, the urn contained the unimaginable riches of the mighty pharaoh, who kept his treasure here to keep it safe from thieves. Other legends tell of daredevils who tried to reach the urn in order

Fig. 47 – The upper floor of the façade of the Treasury.

to seize its riches, all of whom naturally failed and lost their life or health into the bargain. In more recent times (the 19th century), local Bedouins, making use of antiquated guns, attempted to smash or shoot down the urn. The urn survived intact, albeit with bullet marks, and none of the marksmen made their fortune. Nobody dreams of following their example today, but on some drawings made by travellers from the beginning of the 19th century (including those of Leon de Laborde) it is possible to observe local Bedouins aiming at the urn in the hope of obtaining the treasures of the mighty pharaoh.

The Corinthian colonnade surrounding the tholos supports an entablature decorated by a beautiful, vegetal frieze and most probably the heads of the Gorgons (effaced by iconoclasts). This is all crowned by 'broken' gables, on the tops of which the figures of fairly well-preserved eagles can be seen.

Fig. 48 – Central tholos adorning the upper floor of the façade of the Treasury.

Fig. 49 – The bottom floor of the Treasury – the vestibule and entrances to the three internal chambers.

Two other elements can be noted when studying the façade of the Treasury: 'obelisks', which rise out of the upper floor and 'enter' the natural rock above, and two rows of openings cut on both sides of the façade. Concerning the former, we do not know if the effect created was the intention of the artist or if it merely demonstrates the incompleteness of the building. As for the latter, the openings were probably cut to form a kind of rock ladder, which would have allowed stonemasons and artists access to a special temporary platform created for use while building the Treasury.

After being enchanted by the façade of the Pharaoh's Treasury, it is then possible to enter its interior, which represents the polar opposite of the rich splendour of its exterior. On passing through the two central columns, you find yourself in a vestibule **(Fig. 49)** in front of the massive, richly decorated entrance to the main chamber, nearly eight metres in height. To the sides are the somewhat smaller entrances to the side chambers, which are nevertheless equally impressive in size and decoration.

The central chamber was undoubtedly the funerary one, whilst the side ones were probably triclinia, although some researchers believe that they were used by priests to perform ceremonies or rituals of which we do not know the details today. Moving up the steps, you pass through the main entrance, where we can see traces of a massive, fortified double gate, which was probably made of wood. Suddenly, you are in the central chamber of the Treasury, which is empty and nearly entirely bereft of any decoration

(Fig. 50). The only decorations present in this chamber (which has measurements of 11 by 12.5 metres and is 10 metres high) are the entrances to the side rooms (niches) on each of the walls, which we can only assume is where the bodies of the dead would have been placed. The back recess, which is in the shape of a square with sides of 3.4 metres, could have once contained the sarcophagus of the king who was laid to rest here.

Some researchers suggest that the currently smooth walls of the interior were originally covered in plaster and paintings. Proof of this is supposedly found in the fact that practically none of the rock-cut buildings in Petra have totally smooth interior walls. Instead, they possess diagonal, precisely running grooves running parallel to one another, most probably left by the tool which was used to work the wall originally. These grooves would have provided support for the plaster layer, which has, however, not survived to our times. It is not clear where the truth lies, but one thing is certain: even these seemingly bare walls are already extremely decorative in their own right due to the changing colour of the rock and the brilliantly conceived organisation of the tomb within the rock structure itself.

The Pharaoh's Treasury is one of the most mysterious ancient buildings of the Near East. We do not know exactly when it was built, who built it or to whom it was dedicated. Most scholars seem to agree that it was meant for one of the Nabataean kings, although another theory deems it to be a temple of one of the Nabataean gods or even a temple with the tomb of a king who rose to the level of god (perhaps King Obodas). Even more problematic is

Fig. 50 – The main chamber of the Pharaoh's Treasury.

the dating of al-Khazneh. Researchers can only place it within a more than 200 year period from the 1st century BCE to halfway through the 2nd century CE. The lack of any kind of inscription or archaeological finds which could provide an accurate date means a comparative and iconographic approach needs to be taken.

By comparing the style, method of execution and decorative elements with other preserved ancient structures of the Mediterranean region, we are led slowly but surely to Hellenistic Alexandria in Egypt. It is here that the prototype of the Treasury's wondrously beautiful façade can be found in the shape of its ancient art gallery. Its shape was that of a courtyard with a tholos situated in the middle, surrounded by a double portico. The complex was entered through a monumental gate ("*propylaea*"), which is captured in the lower section of the Treasury façade. Statues were placed in both the tholos itself as well as in the portico arcade, a design echoed in the façade decoration of al-Khazneh (this type of 'gallery' is known from Ancient Rome, for example the Porticus of Octavia). Continuing along this line of investigation, one comes to the conclusion that the artisans and artists who created al-Khazneh for one of the Nabataean kings must have come from Alexandria.

The king who ordered the Treasury's construction obviously wanted his building to eclipse all the others built before it in Petra. One of the candidates for this role comes in the shape of King Aretas III (86-62 BCE), who described himself on his coins as *Philhellenos*, meaning 'Lover of Greek art and culture'. Malichus I (60-30 BCE) and Obodas II (30-9 BCE) are other possibilities, but the most likely is surely Aretas IV (9 BCE – 40 CE), under whose rule Nabataean architecture reached its zenith.

A minor excavation conducted by archaeologists underneath the Treasury led to the discovery of a further two funerary chambers decorated by typical Nabataean facades. They may well predate the Treasury itself, although the type of architectonic decoration within them could suggest they appeared later on. The same excavation also confirmed the theory that the level of the Wadi al-Jarra (within which the Treasury was cut) was approximately four metres lower than today in Nabataean times. We still do not know if the Pharaoh's Treasury formed part of a much more elaborate funerary complex (as is the case with the Tomb of the Roman Soldier in the Wadi Farasa), but it seems unlikely. The very architectural conception of the Treasury is already that of a coherent Nabataean funerary complex; the lower columns form the courtyard, the triclinia are present as side chambers and it also possesses a central funerary chamber.

Opposite the Pharaoh's Treasury, it is possible to visit two more rock-cut tombs. The one closer to the exit to the gorge is a Hegr type tomb **(Fig. 51)**.

Fig. 51 – Hegr Tomb opposite the Pharaoh's Treasury.

This is one of the few rock-cut tombs which has been wrought from two sides; the majority were only worked from one. Unfortunately, we do not know the full decoration which the walls of this tomb would once have had, as they have not yet been uncovered to their ancient layer. It is, however, surely one of the later tombs of Petra. Judging from its decoration (e.g. dwarf pilasters), it should be dated to the second half of the 1st century CE.

Located to its left, Tomb No. 64 (according to Domaszewski's numbering) is an example of a Nabataean Hegr façade tomb **(Fig. 52)**, although it is, unfortunately, badly preserved. Archaeological research was carried out on the tomb around 1980. This confirmed that the deceased were placed into the niche cut into the back wall, which is flanked by pilasters, as late as the beginnings of the 4th century CE.

The Wadi Musa turns northwest at the Pharaoh's Treasury. This area

Fig. 52 – Hegr Tomb No. 64.

is commonly known as the Outer Siq and the valley widens as it heads in the direction of the royal necropolis and the Theatre **(Fig. 53)**.

Fig. 53 – Outer Siq. Triclinium No. 65 is on the right.

About 50 metres after leaving the Treasury, an enormous rock recess can be seen to the right. The remains of one of the largest triclinia (feasting hall) are found here. About 20 metres further along, this time to the left, is a façade which may have belonged to a grave which was destroyed by an earthquake **(Fig. 54)**. The remaining fragment presents a podium decorated by geo-

Fig. 54 – Damaged façade of Tomb No. 66.

metric ornamentation, as well as two pilasters with Nabataean capitals. The stylistic decoration probably dates to a relatively late period, most probably the end of the 1st century CE.

About 200 metres along from the Treasury, impressive façade tombs cut in various styles begin to appear on the rock walls of the gorge. At a certain point, you feel as if you are in a bizarre art gallery, the walls of which are ornamented by rock-cut decoration. To the left, three mighty façade tombs stand in a row. These were numbered 67, 68 and 69 by Domaszewski **(Fig. 55)**.

Fig. 55 – Tombs No. 67-70.

The first of these is Tomb No. 67, a beautiful example of a Hegr type tomb **(Fig. 56)**. Its main characteristic feature is the presence of an additional funerary chamber located at its summit between two diverging sets of steps. The chamber is not large (approximately 2.8 by 2.8 metres), but it was certainly the place the deceased were placed. If we observe the walls closely, we can discern the remains of plaster between the rows of steps, which would have been coloured by paint in the past. Although it seems improbable today, a large amount of the rock façades of Petra would once have been plastered and painted in various colours. Whilst observing façade tomb 67, attention should also be paid to the obelisks standing on rectangular bases with are carved into the rock to the right of the main entrance. These symbolised those at rest in the tomb, although we are unlikely to ever know who they may have been. The answer to this question would

Fig. 56 – Hegr Tomb No. 67.

undoubtedly have been provided by signs once affixed above the obelisks, but unfortunately only the openings which were once used to hold them up remain.

Tomb 68 possesses a façade of the pylon type with a double decorative row at the top of the crowstep. A female who was ranked highly in the social hierarchy was most probably placed here. It is interesting to speculate as to whether the funerary chamber was located below today's path level (which would explain the 'step' nature of the tomb's base) or if we are dealing with an unfinished tomb or maybe even a cenotaph. At the bottom of the façade, it is also possible to see an obelisk standing on a rectangular base carved into the stone.

Tomb 69 is again a Hegr type tomb. Although its façade is heavily eroded, one can still clearly observe its additional decoration. This comes in the form of two half columns (topped by Nabataean capitals) that flank the entrance to the funerary chamber and quarter columns, which accompany the side pilasters. Even the entrance to the tomb itself is richly adorned by a double frame. The outer frame, which is better preserved, supports a classical Doric entablature as well as a triangular gable. This type of decoration only appeared relatively late in the second half of the 1st century CE. Looking inside, we discover three niches, which would have once contained the dead.

In this gallery of rock façades, Tomb 70 manages to stand out **(Fig. 57)**. This near freestanding construction (connected to the rock wall on only one side) is unique in all of Petra. Despite the unusually rich decoration of the tomb, which would suggest it being of the Hegr type, it is not topped by diverging steps ascending outwards. These are replaced by a four-level row of crowstep (reminiscent of the pylon type), which creates a type of balustrade that reaches to the top of the tomb on three sides. The lack of an entrance to the funerary chamber is also worth pondering, especially considering the fact that two of its sides bear the rich frame decoration which would normally have surrounded one. It cannot be ruled out that tomb 70 is, like tomb 68, an unfinished one or perhaps it only served the purpose of a cenotaph. Whilst admiring tomb 70, attention should also be turned to the 'blind' entrance on the northern side. On top of the triangular gable, it is possible to see the remains of the figure which once adorned it. Could it have been Isis seated on a throne? Or perhaps the goddess Tyche standing with her cornucopia? Unfortunately, due to its poor state of preservation, we will never know.

Continuing towards the centre of Petra, we pass another rock tomb to our left, this time of the pylon type, which has unfortunately been badly damaged by an earthquake. To the right, however, we can now see a series of six tomb façades which are placed higher and higher as we go along. Originally there were seven, but the first

Fig. 57 – Hegr Tomb No. 70.

and lowest of these was destroyed by an earthquake, although some of its remains can be seen sticking out of the ground. The next five façades are of the pylon type. Interestingly, some of the higher rows of crowstep of these tombs were built on top rather than carved out of the wall. The last of this group of graves, which is of Hegr type, was given the number 825 by Domaszewski and is also known as the Tomb of the 17 Graves (**Fig. 58**). This name originates from the number of niches where the dead were buried which were uncovered here during archaeological investigation. Fourteen of these are located within the floor of the tomb, whilst the three remaining ones were cut into the back wall. To the left of the entrance, it is also possible to observe five obelisks standing on decorated base foundations carved into the wall. On two of these bases, a preserved inscription can be seen mentioning the dead sons and grandsons of Yaqim, who were laid to rest in this tomb. In front of the tomb is a recess with two benches

Fig. 58 – Tombs No. 822-825. The Tomb of the 17 Graves is on the left.

which once must have performed the function of a biclinium, the place where funerary meals were consumed.

Standing and facing the group of façades just mentioned, you will see a water channel running above, which delivers water to the centre of Petra. It is cut into the rock above the 'lower' tombs (steps leading up to it have even been preserved), but in the case of the two highest it has been thoughtfully

Fig. 59 – The Outer Siq looking towards the Theatre.

cut so as to be incorporated into their previously existing façades. Fragments of 'little bridges', which covered the gap between the tombs, have also survived to the present day.

Very close nearby is a place where the rock gorge opens out fully. In front, the auditorium of the Theatre can already be made out in the distance **(Fig. 59)**. On the left, there are steps leading to the peak of Jabal Madbah, where the most important cult place of the Nabataeans, the High Place of Sacrifice (see Trail 5), is located.

After the steps and before the Theatre, on the north-eastern side of Jabal Madbah, a series of façade graves positioned in four rows, which are accurately termed the Streets of Façades, leap to your attention **(Fig. 60)**. These tombs mostly date to the earliest period of rock façade construction in Petra and allow us to track the development of the form and decoration of Nabataean sepulchral architecture. Simple pylon tombs are the most numerous with either one or two row of crowstep friezes. A few step, proto-Hegr and Hegr types can also be seen, as well as some rarely encountered arch tombs. The fact that the majority of these tombs lack any kind of classical decoration, such as for example a framed entrance with a Doric entablature supporting a triangular gable, should be noted. Pure Nabataean forms dominate here, which surely indicates that the tombs were created before the time

Fig. 60 – The Streets of Façades.

of Hellenic borrowing in Nabataean art and architecture. Somewhat further along in the direction of the Theatre we can see 31 more tombs, this time cut along just two 'streets'.

To the right, on the south-western slope of al-Khubtha and opposite the Streets of Façades, the necropolis of royal officials **(Fig. 61)** begins. This later turns into the stunning royal necropolis, which majestically rises out over the extensive valley of Petra. The royal necropolis is so named due to its group of impressive tombs of the Roman Temple type (according to Domaszewski's typology), which must have belonged to Nabataean leaders and members of the royal family. A description of the individual tombs can be found in Trail 4, which covers the Royal Tombs.

Fig. 61 – South-western slope of al-Khubtha. The necropolis of the royal officials.

The tomb furthest to the south of the necropolis of royal officials is the Tomb of Uneishu **(Fig. 62)**, which lies above the previously described Tomb of the 17 Graves and directly opposite the Streets of Façades. Thanks to an inscription found in it as early as the 19th century, it is one of the few tombs in Petra of which we know the name of the owner. Uneishu was probably an official (something like a prime-minister today) in the court of Shuqailat II, the wife of King Malichus II (40-70 CE). This queen ruled as regent for several years after the death of her husband, on behalf of her son and heir to the throne, Rabbel II (70-106 CE), who was not yet of age.

The façade of this tomb, which is situated on a small platform, has the characteristic appearance of a Nabataean Hegr type tomb with two side pilasters

Fig. 62 – Tomb of Uneishu (No. 813).

supporting a double entablature topped by an attic with steps diverging from each other and ascending outwards. The decoration of the entrance consists of outer pilasters supporting a double architrave, which is topped by a cornice. The interior frame is formed by pillars created though a combination of pilasters and quarter columns with Nabataean capitals. These bear an architrave crowned by a triangular gable. Three consoles under the acroterion complete the decoration. Eleven niches are cut inside the tomb, where the dead would have been placed. Apart from Uneishu himself, other members of his family were also buried here in the second half of the 1st century CE.

The Tomb of Uneishu is of additional interest as it is a rare example of a complete Nabataean funerary complex. An open courtyard is cut out of the rock and surrounded by porticos on two sides (which unfortunately have not survived to our times) and both water cisterns and a triclinium are also present. The entrance to the latter is found in the northern side of the courtyard to the left of the funerary chamber if we are stood facing it. The triclinium had measurements of approximately 7 by 10 metres and in later times (the 3rd-4th centuries CE) was definitely used as a tomb. This is demonstrated by the niches cut into its back wall.

The tomb can either be reached by a poorly demarcated, steep path which leads directly to its base or by a considerably easier (but longer) one which leads to it via The Urn Tomb (see Trail 4).

Continuing on towards the Theatre, another very well-preserved Hegr type tomb (Tomb 808) can be seen to the right. Its decoration is similar to that of the Tomb of Uneishu, but its facade is of slightly bigger size. Behind it, other façades of various types are situated, the most interesting of which are (pylon) Tomb 780 and (Hegr) Tomb 778 **(Fig. 63)**.

Fig. 63 – Tombs of the royal officials: No. 780 (left), No. 778 (upper middle).

After another 50 metres or so we finally come to the Theatre **(Fig. 64)**. Already at first glance, it is clear that the building interrupts the course of the necropolis which once stood here. Indeed, if we look up, it is clear to see that the cutting of the auditorium must have involved the destruction of tombs which were previously placed there, as parts of their funerary chambers can still be seen today in the form of rock niches. Some of the travellers who visited Petra in the 19th century misconstrued these as loge seating for honourable persons, almost certainly as a result of comparison with other contemporary theatres known to them.

It was originally thought that the Petra Theatre was only created in Roman times (after 106 CE) and that it was the only Roman contribution to the architectural development of the city. It was only in the 1960s that research carried out by American archaeologists showed that the Theatre, despite the fact that it was constructed following the precepts of Roman architecture, was actually built as early as the times of King Aretas IV (in the period between 4 BCE and 27 CE), when the rock-cut city was at its economic peak. It was, however, rebuilt twice in later times, the first time under the reign of King Malichus II (40-70 CE) and the second after the Romans assumed control of Petra in 106 CE. The Theatre was then completely destroyed by

Fig. 64 – The Theatre. View from the top of al-Khubtha.

the powerful earthquake which struck in 363 CE. Parts of it were later used in the construction of other complexes in the Byzantine period.

The Theatre can be entered from the Wadi Musa side through two rock-cut passages (*vomitoriae*), which are found either side of the auditorium. The auditorium of the theatre itself (*theatron*), which was intended for between seven and eight thousand spectators, was also nearly entirely cut out of rock; only a few parts on its sides were built onto the rock. The viewing area **(Fig. 65)** was divided horizontally into three sections (*summa, media* and *ima cavea*) that were separated by two small aisles (*praecinctiones*). Forty rows of seats were accessible on seven steep and narrow levels, which started from the level of the orchestra. The orchestra was semicircular with a diameter of about 25 metres. It was created by flattening the rock level and then covering it with a layer of hard cement. A stage (*pulpitum*), over six metres wide and 50 metres long, rose in front of the orchestra. It could be reached via two sets of steps with a width of one-and-a-half metres. The stage was laid with calcareous slabs, which rested on a specially created framework (still visible today). The background for spectacles onstage was created by a stage

Fig. 65 – The Theatre. View from the audience towards the stage. The Wadi Musa is in the background.

building (*scaenae frons*), which probably reached to a height of 18 metres (in Roman theatres, its height was usually the same of that of the top row of seats). It must have been richly decorated with architectonic elements such as columns (including Nabataean columns) and niches. Statues must also have been placed within it (archaeologists have found fragments of statues of Hercules and Aphrodite amongst others), just as was the case in the marvellous Roman theatre of Bosra (Syria). Today it is hard to imagine, but in Nabataean and Roman times it would have been impossible to see the rows of seating of the auditorium from the road leading along the Wadi Musa. The view would have been completely cut off by the imposing stage background.

Above the rock wall over the auditorium, it is possible to see the remains of one of the main channels which delivered water to the centre of Petra. In the rock recesses, the tombs which managed to survive the preparation of the terrain for the building of the Theatre are also visible.

The seemingly barbaric act of destroying pre-existing façade tombs in order to construct a theatre has great significance for us. Thanks to it, we can state with complete confidence (as we know the date of construction of the Theatre) that the tombs from the necropolis surrounding the Theatre (both surviving and destroyed) come from the 1st century BCE, almost certainly from its beginning, as the destruction of façades which had just been built seems highly unlikely. This represents a key piece of the puzzle which archaeologists who are wrestling with the question of dating Nabataean façade graves have to deal with.

Continuing along the Wadi Musa, which turns to the north at the theatre, we pass a few more tombs to our left, nearly all of which are entirely rock-cut. On the right, there are vast complexes of rooms, sometimes fantastically decorated by the natural colour of the rock, the usage of which has not yet been satisfactorily established **(Fig. 66)**. Some believe them to have been living quarters (similar to the House of Dorotheos on the western slope of

Fig. 66 – Rock-cut rooms opposite the Theatre.

al-Khubtha – see Trail 7), whilst others stress their location right next to the most important necropolis of Petra (the royal necropolis). The latter argument suggests that the most sensible answer to this question is that these complexes were either shops or storehouses. The adjacent theatre also counts in favour of their possible significance to trade.

Trail 1 finishes with the steps leading to the royal necropolis visible to the right. The visit can be continued either in the direction of the City Centre (Trail 2) or in the direction of the mighty rock-cut Royal Tombs (Trail 4).

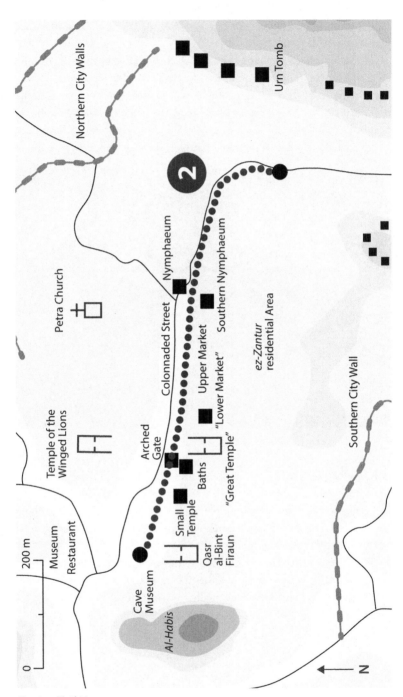

Fig. 67 – Trail No. 2.

The City Centre (South): The Colonnaded Street – The Great Temple – Qasr al-Bint Firaun Temple (Fig. 67)

Trail 2 is a natural continuation of Trail 1. On this trail, there are no tricky climbs, but at the beginning there is an awkward, sandy road. It must also be pointed out that this trail is practically entirely on open terrain, meaning that it could be tough in summer in the early afternoon due to the heat of the sun. The trail should take approximately two hours (there and back).

Wandering further along the bottom of the Wadi Musa valley from the Theatre, we soon see the magnificent façades of the monumental tombs which are considered to be the resting places of the Nabataean kings. Information concerning them can be found in Trail 4, which covers the Royal Tombs.

In front of the first royal tomb (the Urn Tomb), the Wadi Musa takes a 90 degree turn to the west. This is where the centre of ancient Petra begins **(Fig. 68)**.

Fig. 68 – The city centre of Petra.

This was also the start of the main (and therefore most celebrated) road of the city, which ran in an east to west direction and is currently known as the Colonnaded Street. Along both sides of it, the most eye-catching public buildings, such as temples, were erected. Before reaching the preserved section of the paved Colonnaded Street, we should turn our attention (at its eastern end on the right (northern) side) to a set of remains lying in the shade of the highest tree in the area, which would once have formed a semicircular Nymphaeum **(Fig. 69)**. This was the city fountain, which was dedicated to water nymphs. It was similar in design to many examples of the type known from other Hellenistic and Roman sites (a wonderfully

Fig. 69 – The Nymphaeum.

preserved nymphaeum can be admired in ancient Gerasa (today Jeresh) in Jordan). Unfortunately, since archaeological research has yet to be carried out here, we neither know when the Petraean Nymphaeum was built nor what it actually looked like.

Opposite the fountain, on the other side of the path, the ruins of another building are to be found. The remnants of its front columns are still visible. One theory suggests it to be the Southern Nymphaeum **(Fig. 70)**, but it is also possible that they are the remains of a smaller temple lying at the entrance to the city centre.

Moving further west, we pass monumental steps leading to the Upper Market on our left **(Fig. 71)**. But where did this name originate? If we look from above at the terrain lying to the south of the Colonnaded Street, we

Fig. 70 – The 'Southern Nymphaeum'.

can make out three rectangular empty spaces. Three German researchers (W. Bachman, T. Wiegand and C. Watzinger) were the first to identify
and interpret these 'courtyards' in 1921. They believed that they were once
the Nabataean trading centres of Petra, a city which existed and prospered
mainly from trade and commerce. These scholars assigned names to these
three courtyards, or 'markets', and they were thus identified as 'upper', 'cen-

Fig. 71 – Monumental steps leading to the Upper Market.

tral' and 'lower'. Their assumption was not based on the results of archaeological research, but on their intuition, which told them that these great, wide open spaces must have served as centres of trade, or *agorae*. Since no excavation work had been conducted here, the view that they were used for trading purposes, as well as their naming as 'markets', perpetuated until the end of the 20th century. It was only in 2009 that American archaeologists from Brown University started to conduct the first archaeological survey of the Upper Market site, which was supported by geophysical prospecting of the terrain. This investigation discovered that (at least in the northern part, nearest the Colonnaded Street) the land had been paved and that underneath it there was a complicated hydrotechnical system, which both stored water (a massive cistern) and transported it (underground channels). Since no freestanding buildings have so far been discovered here (e.g. temples), it seems that we are indeed dealing with an expansive courtyard, perhaps something in the style of the Roman forum or the Hellenistic agora. Below the steps leading to the Upper Market, a fragment of an inscription was also found, thanks to which we know that a victory arch dedicated to Emperor Trajan in 114 CE once stood here.

The preserved section of the Colonnaded Street is six metres wide and 250 metres long **(Fig. 72)**. This main artery of Petra (*cardo*) was paved with flat

Fig. 72 – The Colonnaded Street – cardo.

stone slabs, which were larger and more regular to the east and smaller and more varied to the west. Along both sides of the road, a pavement ran at an elevation of two steps, on which the columns with Ionic capitals which give the road its modern name stood.

Some of the columns were raised and reconstructed over the course of renovation work conducted around 1960 **(Fig. 73)**. According to archaeo-

Fig. 73 – Raised columns of the cardo.

logical research, the stone paving of the Colonnaded Street should be dated either to the end of the 1st century BCE or to the beginning of the 1st century CE. It was also established that there were traces of winding tracks underneath the sections of paved street which can still be seen today. These came from as early as the end of the 4th century or the beginning of the 3rd century BCE. This has been recently confirmed by archaeologists working in the *Early Petra Project*. Thanks to their work, we can now state that the beginnings of the *cardo*, or Colonnaded Street, date all the way back to the 4th century BCE.

Next to the steps leading to the Upper Market, our attention should also turn to the remains of some smaller rooms, probably shops, which date to the period between the 1st century CE and Byzantine times. One of the inscriptions discovered on their outer wall contained a dedication to the Emperor Diocletian, which dates to approximately 283 CE. Opposite the shops and the columns of the southern portico standing in front of them, we can see the Wadi Musa riverbed (altered in modern times) to the north (right) and behind it the ruins of a building deemed to be a Byzantine fortress.

Continuing along the main thoroughfare of Petra, it is worth turning around now and again to admire the beautifully crafted façade tombs of the royal necropolis, which are clearly visible from here.

To the south (left) of the western end of the Colonnaded Street, stand the imposing remains of a complex described in literature as the South or Great Temple, to which some reconstructed steps lead **(Fig. 74)**. American

Fig. 74 – The Great Temple Complex.

archaeologists from Brown University have been researching this complex since 1993 and their work of over 20 years has furnished us with incredibly valuable information concerning the whole complex. At the same time, however, it has also raised many new questions to which we do not yet have satisfactory answers. All we can do is wait for their next discovery, which will form another piece of the solution to this intriguing puzzle.

The complex of the Great Temple is undoubtedly one of the most important sites in Petra **(Fig. 75)**. It covers an area of 7,650 square metres, which makes it the largest archaeological construction which has been investigated in Petra so far. It runs from north to south and is made up of three main parts: a propylaea (monumental entrance), a lower temenos (surrounded on two sides by a triple colonnade) and an upper temenos (on which the main building of the whole complex once stood).

Fig. 75 – Layout of the Great Temple Complex.

As it was in the past, the propylaea now also serves as the main entrance to the complex from the side of the Colonnaded Street. After passing through it, we come to the lower temenos. It is a vast courtyard and its floor was laid with bright, hexagonal, limestone slabs, which covered an elaborate underground hydrotechnical system. The courtyard has measurements of 49 by 56 metres. To its eastern and western sides, the columns of the abovementioned triple portico stand. At the southern end of the portico are semicircular exedrae, which have two columns standing at their entrance. The eastern (to the left when looking from the entrance) exedra is of more interest, as it contains the remains of a relief decoration which would have presented busts of different gods (including Tyche/Fortuna). Near to the western exedra, archaeologists came across a remarkable capital decorated by the heads of elephants (in the Asian style) in the first years of their investigation. Similar capitals were then discovered in other parts of the lower temenos **(Fig. 76)**. It therefore seems that most (if not all) of the capitals of the triple portico were once decorated by precisely this type of design, unique among all the rock structures of the whole of the Near East.

Monumental steps lead from the lower temenos to the upper, which are situated next to the eastern and western exedrae. Those on the eastern side are currently blocked by the fallen columns of the main building complex. The western steps, which we can still make use of, lead us to a small courtyard in front of the temple, which is flanked to the east and west by three-and-a-half metre wide passages.

Fig. 76 – Capital decorated with the heads of elephants found at the Great Temple Complex (now in the Petra Archaeological Museum).

Research conducted thus far has allowed archaeologists to identify as many as fourteen phases of construction of the Great Temple. Phase 0 is the period before the building of the temple. The next, dating to the beginnings of the 1st century BCE (Phase 1), represents the time when the land was being prepared for the construction of the complex and the underground hydrotechnical system was being put in place. Phase 2, which dates to about halfway through the 1st century BCE, saw the construction of the main basis of the complex, as well as that of the central building. This earliest temple (measuring 18.36 by 30 metres) was erected in the *distilos in antis* form, meaning a construction with two columns in the façade, which stand between the antae. At their widest, the antae were formed of eight columns, whilst at the back there were six. All were topped by magnificent Corinthian capitals. Their angular supports were also highly interesting, as they were formed by a rectangular pillar with two connected half columns. This was all surrounded by outer walls, which contained nine entrances, three on each side. Between the walls and the colonnade, there were narrow corridors. Unfortunately, we do not know what the interior of the building would have looked like at this time, because it was completely rebuilt in later periods. Both the columns and the walls of the building were covered in plaster and decorated in a manner reminiscent of Pompeiian styles I and II.

Phase 4 witnessed the first development of the temple and dates to the beginning of the Common Era. This was part of the building activity carried out by Aretas IV. At this time, (on the entrance side) he built a kind of vestibule (*pronaos*) onto the previous façade in the *tetrastilos in antis* style (four columns between the antae), which contained paved eastern and western passages. After this extension was completed, the temple had measurements of 35.5 by 42.5 metres and the columns (of a diameter of 1.5 metres) included into the façade reached a height of 15 metres. We do not know if the building was covered by a roof, although it seems unlikely. Apart from the temple itself, the rest of the complex was also further developed. The mighty propylaea construction with a central entrance (which led to the lower temenos) was erected and then lower temenos was covered with hexagonal slabs. Next, on both sides of it, triple porticos were built. The two exedrae and the rear section of the complex (the living quarters, the 'baroque' rooms and the great cistern) were also created at this time.

The most important alteration from an archaeological point of view occurred in Phase 5 (1st century CE), when the whole complex was completely rebuilt. The most important alterations were made to the main building, which converted it into an auditorium (*theatron*) with a capacity of 620 **(Fig. 77)**. This surrounded a semicircular orchestra (with a diameter of 6.4 metres), in front of which stood a small stage (*pulpitum*). In order to provide support for the auditorium, the empty space between the columns was filled in and special, curved rooms were constructed. These rooms held up the system of steps which allowed access to the higher rows of seats built towards the back of the auditorium. The auditorium was divided into four sections (*cunei*), which were themseves divided by three sets of stairs (*scalaria*).

The next two phases (Phase 6 and Phase 7) date to the Roman period (after 106 CE). Nothing was done to alter the architecture of the complex except

Fig. 77 – Theatron in the Great Temple.

for a few essential repairs and occasional reconstruction work, for example after earthquakes. From the end of the 2nd century CE (Phase 8), the complex began to fall into ruin. Its story probably ends, alongside that of most of the other Nabataean-Roman constructions of Petra, with the great earthquake of 363 CE (Phase 9). Over the following centuries up to the present day (Phases 10-14), the remains were only used for short periods of time as living quarters.

In the 1990s, archaeologists were greatly shocked to discover the remains of a theatre within the temple, as no other 'temple-theatre' had previously been discovered anywhere else. Perhaps, however, we should not consider the building known as the Great Temple to be a sacred one at all. Indeed, it would presently appear that the complex was a secular construction from the beginning, as this seems far more probable than the theory propounded by some researchers that it was initially a temple which was then converted into a secular building. Perhaps this building was a basilica originally, where people met to conduct transactions and settle business disputes. Then, as it took on the form of a theatron, it could have become a kind of bouleuterion (the place where the city council would have convened). Still other researchers believe it was part of a royal palace.

After familiarising ourselves with the history of this mysterious building, it is worth taking a short walk around its outer walls. On the eastern side, it is possible to see the reconstructed eastern perimeter wall. Whilst approaching it, we pass the opening of a great cistern (with measurements of 7.8 by 8.5 metres and a height of 5.88 metres), which would have stored nearly 330,000 litres of water. Continuing on, you can search for the figure considered to be

a sword-god in the rock face above the southern wall, which was dedicated to the Nabataean god, Dushara **(Fig. 78)**.

A little further on, between the back wall of the temple and the southern wall, there is an entrance to the series of so-called 'baroque' rooms. This name was attributed to them because of their extraordinarily rich decoration. In one of them, an extremely beautiful stucco (plaster) decorated ceiling can be found, which has been partly reconstructed by archaeologists, despite the fact that it had fallen to the floor. After

Fig. 78 – The Sword-God.

the baroque rooms, the partly dug-up living quarters can be seen, which date to the 1st century CE. On our return journey it is also possible to scale the outer back steps of the temple to view the theatral auditorium/odeon built within from above.

On returning to the lower temenos, it is worth taking a moment to look at the open and almost empty space to its east. This is the Lower Market mentioned above **(Fig. 79)**. Due to its location between the complex of the Great Temple and the residential area of ez-Zantur, it can be assumed that this place played an important role in the life of the city. In spite of this fact, it was only in 1998 that the first archaeological investigation was carried out

Fig. 79 – The 'Lower Market'. The 'Building on the Water' is visible in the foreground.

here, which brought both shocking and unexpected results. The remains of a great open water tank (or basin) were discovered here (with measurements of 23 by 43 metres and a depth of 2.5 metres). It was found in the southern part of the Lower Market and a small building rose from its centre.

In order to construct this 'building on the water', it was necessary to cut a mighty stone shelf (32 by 65 metres) into the rock, which is now called the Southern Terrace. The depth of this hollow reaches up to 16 metres in some places. This was then extended to the north by 53 metres, creating an area now termed the Northern Terrace. Between the north and south terraces, a two-and-a-half metre high retaining wall was constructed, which divided the whole area of the Lower Market into two parts **(Fig. 80)**. The southern part (Southern Terrace) contained the massive water tank previ-

Fig. 80 – Retaining wall (in the middle) separating the two sections of the 'Lower Market'.

ously mentioned. In the middle of the 'lake', a small pavilion of 11.5 by 14.5 metres (with wide entrances to the north, east and west) was erected on an artificial, rectangular island. The decorated framing of the entrances was similar to those of certain façade tombs and the interior was richly decorated by stucco and paintings, traces of which have been discovered during excavations. It probably also contained four columns supporting a ceiling, although the possibility also exists that this structure was not covered by a roof.

Over the course of further investigation, the remains of a complex, underground hydrotechnical system connecting the tank to the Northern Terrace were discovered. Since no traces of a larger building have been found in this northern section, it has been suggested that this was in fact a garden which incorporated the adjacent artificial lake. This would fit the account of Strabo, who described Petra as a city of many water sources (referring to the cisterns), which provided water to houses and gardens. The way into this oasis of greenery would undoubtedly have proceeded from the side of the Great Temple through the eastern triple colonnade (mentioned above) which connected these two architectural constructions. Leigh-Ann Bedal, who is currently researching the 'water complex' area, believes that it was probably created under the rule of Aretas IV around the end of the 1st century BCE, which would coincide with the dating of the period of development of the Great Temple. Later, after the Roman annexation of Nabataea, the complex was renovated. But what function could this 'water complex' have performed in Nabataean and Roman

Petra? It must have been an area for relaxation, perhaps only accessible to the kings and their court or perhaps to all citizens. The coolness of the blue water and luscious plant vegetation must have created an oasis of calm far removed from the burning sun and daily hustle and bustle of the rock-cut city.

But let us return to the Colonnaded Street once more, which was completed on the western side by an imposing gate with three passageways leading through it. Before we consider the gate itself, attention should be paid to the steps on the left (southern) side, which would have formed the entrance to the Great Temple complex before the construction of the monumental propylaea. If you choose to ascend them, you will find yourself standing before a bathing complex, constructed after the Roman annexation of Petra in 106 CE, which is built along the lines of a typical Roman bath **(Fig. 81)**. Its centre was formed by a broad palaestra, from which a corridor led to the *apoditerium* (changing room) and then to the bathing rooms themselves: the *frigidarium*, *tepidarium* and *caldarium*.

Fig. 81 – Roman Baths located next to the Great Temple Complex.

On returning to the Colonnaded Street, we are confronted by a massive structure now known as the Arched Gate **(Fig. 82)**. Its appearance and arrangement calls to mind a Roman victory arch, such as the magnificent Hadrian Arch located in the nearby ancient city of Gerasa (today Jeresh). The Arched Gate leads to an expansive temenos (sacred precinct), which encircles the Qasr al-Bint Firaun temple. As was proven by excavation work conducted here in the 1950s by a British archaeological team led by Peter

Fig. 82 – The Arched Gate.

Parr, the Arched Gate visible today was constructed just after the paving of the Colonnaded Street, probably at the end of the 1st or the beginning of the 2nd century CE. It was erected on a site where an earlier gate had once stood, undoubtedly built towards the end of the 1st century BCE. As mentioned above, there were three passageways through this arch, of which the central one was larger than the side ones. From the Colonnaded Street side, the passageways were flanked by freestanding columns, which were positioned on pedestals which leant slightly forward. To the west, however, half columns were used as decoration instead of columns.

The Arched Gate was richly adorned with small panels bearing sculpted ornamentation of geometric shapes, vegetation and even images of gods (the latter have unfortunately been largely destroyed by iconoclasts), some of which have survived to the present day. Archaeologists have also discovered the bust of either the Nabataean god, Dushara, or the Egyptian Serapis, which would probably once have crowned the top of the Arched Gate (**Fig. 83**). Today, it can be viewed in a museum which is located in a modern building in the centre of Petra.

To the north and south of the gate, we can make out the remains of two structures resembling towers, the usage of which has not yet been agreed upon, although certain researchers connect them to religious ceremonies (the details of which we do not know) taking place within the sacred precinct (temenos). Behind the ruins of the southern 'tower' are the remains of three rooms, covered by ceilings, which are considered to be Byzantine baths.

After passing through the Arched Gate, let us turn our attention to a small, recently discovered building located past and above it to the south (left), which was probably a Roman temple dedicated to divine emperors **(Fig. 84)**. It can be reached by a path fairly well-trodden by tourists. During research conducted here under S. K. Reid, American archaeologists established that the temple, which was built in the 2nd century CE, stood on a low

Fig. 83 – Bust of the Nabataean god, Dushara, or the Egyptian god, Serapis, found near the Arched Gate (now in the Archaeological Museum of Petra).

platform and could be reached via steps leading from the temenos. It was fronted by a small vestibule, the façade of which was adorned by six columns crowned by Corinthian capitals. The cella of the temple was built in the

Fig. 84 – The Roman Temple dedicated to divine emperors.

shape of a square with sides of 14.62 metres. Its interior contained podiums, on which statues of Roman emperors would once have been placed.

To the west of the Arched Gate, a temenos (sacred precinct) extends out, which was once entirely paved with calcareous slabs. Its measurements are 100 by 180 metres and it runs from east to west. During research conducted here in the 1960s, archaeologists discovered a large number of sculptures and bas-reliefs which once would have decorated central Petra. Some of these architectonic decorations are visible just after the Arched Gate (on the left), whilst the remainder can be viewed at the Archaeological Museum of Amman **(Fig. 85)**.

Fig. 85 – Bas-relief depicting Melpomene found within the temenos of Petra (now in the Archaeological Museum of Amman).

The temenos surrounds the most important temple of Nabataean Petra, Qasr al-Bint Firaun, which in Arabic means "The Castle of the Pharoah's Daughter" **(Fig. 86)**. The name derives from a local Bedouin legend about the imprisoned daughter of a cruel Egyptian leader. The Qasr al-Bint temple is the only freestanding building of Nabataean Petra to remain in such excellent condition, although archaeologists are not entirely sure when it was built. There was already a construction on this spot in the 4th century BCE, although this would certainly have just been living quarters. Later, in the 2nd century BCE, a special platform was built here, on which religious rituals were enacted in honour of the gods. The building visible today was constructed in the 1st century BCE, although we do not know exactly

Fig. 86 – Qasr al-Bint Firaun – the Castle of the Pharaoh's Daughter.

when. The similarity of some of its architectonic detail to the Pharaoh's Treasury suggests the period of rule of Aretas III or Malichus I, but the majority of researchers consider Obodas III to have been the king who oversaw the construction of Qasr al-Bint. Under the rule of Aretas IV, the temple was renovated and this probably occurred again after the Roman annexation of Petra in the 2nd century CE. It was then destroyed in the earthquake of 363 CE.

The temple of Qasr al-Bint is made of local sandstone blocks in the shape of a square (with 32 metre sides), whilst its preserved part reaches a height of 23 metres. It stands on a platform three metres high and monumental steps once led up to it from the north. It consists of a broad vestibule (*pronaos*) and a cella, inside which three adytons can be found at the back. The façade of the vestibule was formed by a portico in antis consisting of four columns with a diameter of two metres and a height of over seventeen, topped by magnificent Corinthian capitals. At its back was an imposing passageway, topped by an arch, which led to the cella. Along its southern wall, meanwhile, were three rooms performing the function of adytons **(Fig. 87)**. In

Fig. 87 – Interior of the temple of Qasr al-Bint Firaun.

the central adyton, on a platform about 1.4 metres high, a stone betyl symbolising the god to whom the temple was dedicated stood on a gold-plated base (as a Byzantine source informs us). In the side adytons, there are steps which once led up to the mezzanine and roof, both of which have not survived to our times.

Qasr al-Bint Firaun's exterior was richly decorated. This included a Doric frieze (which ran between the architrave and cornice), antae and pilasters (adorned by geometric ornamentation) and square panels made of stucco (which graced the lower sections of all of the walls of the building). The exterior décor was completed by pilasters in each of the corners of the temple. Qasr al-Bint was most probably dedicated to the most important god of the Nabataeans, Dushara, who was later identified with Zeus. It could also have been a cult place for other gods, most probably al-Uzza and Allat, which is suggested by the side adytons and a later inscription mentioning Aphrodite (the Greek equivalent of al-Uzza).

In front of the temple, we can see a large, rectangular construction with measurements of 10.8 by 12 metres and a height of 2.25 metres. These are the remains of an altar **(Fig. 88)** on which rituals were performed to the gods who were worshipped in Qasr al-Bint. Investigation of the area by British and French archaeologists has led to the further discovery of an exedra located to the west of the altar. This contained marble statues of Roman emperors, including Marcus Aurelius (whose statue's head was excellently preserved).

Fig. 88 – The altar in front of the temple of Qasr al-Bint Firaun.

The main tourist route of Petra (Trails 1 and 2) finishes at Qasr al-Bint. Most tourists go from here to visit two small museums and to familiarise themselves with their collections, which are modest, but still worth seeing. These collections are soon to be moved to the planned new museum, which will be erected in the vicinity of the tourist centre.

One of the current museums is located in rooms which were cut by Nabataeans into the rock of al-Habis, above the temenos of the Qasr al-Bint temple. Here, it is mainly possible to see fragments of marble statues and architectonic detail, but there are also smaller objects such as ceramic vessels, oil lamps and fragments of terracotta figures. From the terrace in front of the museum, there is a splendid view of the centre of Petra, in particular of the temenos of the Qasr al-Bint temple, the Arched Gate and the Colonnaded Street.

The second museum occupies several rooms in a small tourist complex, where there is also a restaurant and souvenir shop. Among the exhibits presented, we can see an excellently preserved capital decorated by elephant heads from the lower temenos of the Great Temple, as well as several fragments of marble statues found in Petra (including Aphrodite and Hermes). The wonderful thin-walled Nabataean pottery and lamps, as well as the bronze and ivory objects, are also worth a look.

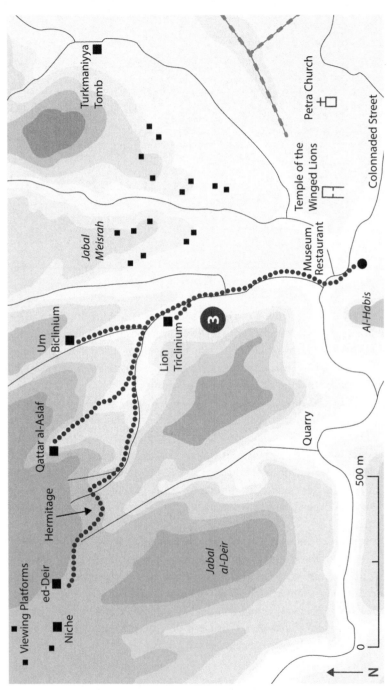

Fig. 89 – Trail No. 3.

TRAIL 3

Wadi ed-Deir – The Monastery (Fig. 89)

One of the most popular routes from the centre of Petra is a walk following the Nabataean processional way along the Wadi ed-Deir which ends at the Monastery (in Arabic "ed-Deir"), one of the largest and most impressive rock buildings of Petra. It begins with a sand track and then turns into a rocky path, which in some places is very narrow. It continues with a steep, winding climb up steps cut by Nabataeans, which includes frequent terrifying drops off precipices into stone abysses. It is worth heading in this direction (it should not take longer than two to three hours to go there and back), however, as ed-Deir itself, as well as the views afforded by the plateau on which it is built, will stay long in the memory.

The walk begins right next to the museum in central Petra, from which we head north. It starts on a difficult, sandy path, which passes by individual rock-cut façades worthy of admiration. These are located both in the valley itself and on the slopes of the M'eisrah mountains (visible to the right). On the left, we pass the remains of rock-cut houses and storehouses, where the local Bedouins have set up parking lots for the camels of today (the most common breeds are Toyota and Isuzu). After about five minutes, we come to a rock path, which soon starts to climb steeply upwards. To our left, we can soon see a small wadi which leads off towards the Lion Triclinium **(Fig. 90)**. The name derives from two reliefs presenting these royal beasts, which flank an entrance to the feasting hall. However, we will never know whether they symbolised one of the gods (for example

Fig. 90 – The Lion Triclinium with the rock-cut betyl on the left.

al-Uzza) or simply were there for decorative purposes. Standing in front of the triclinium façade, let us pay attention to the richness of the decorative elements: richly adorned Corinthian capitals on side pillars consisting of pilasters and quarter columns, a triangular gable crowned by three urns, and a triglyph-metope frieze, of which the outlying metopes on the pillars present the heads of the Gorgons. The whole is completed by a richly decorated tympanum gable, which unfortunately is poorly preserved. Stylistically, the façade of the triclinium can be dated to the second half of the 1st century CE.

To the left of the triclinium façade is a rock-cut betyl, which for certain symbolises the god, Dushara. A little further to the left, two façade tombs are visible. They once would have been richly decorated, but can now only be distinguished by the pilasters which once adorned them. Nevertheless, let us focus on the tomb to the left. Above its entrance, the negatives of friezes and a gable can be made out. This façade would doubtless have once been decorated by architectonic elements made in stucco, but unfortunately they have fallen from the walls and thus have not been preserved to the present day.

If for some reason you miss the Lion Triclinium, it is possible to see it once again to the left of the path just after passing through a fallen piece of rock.

Climbing further upwards, at the moment when the Wadi ed-Deir turns west (left), we can leave the main path for a moment to continue further northwards along the Wadi Khararib. This leads us to one of the best preserved biclinia, known as the Wadi Khararib Biclinium (**Fig. 91**), which

Fig. 91 – Wadi Khararib Biclinium.

is cut out of the rock to our right. Its unusually well-preserved façade is decorated with side pillars, topped by Nabataean capitals, which support a smooth entablature and triangular gable.

Continuing along the Wadi ed-Deir, we have to contend with an ever steeper ascent. At another turn of the steps to the west (left), a barely visible path leads north to Qattar al-Aslaf **(Fig. 92)**. This means 'lower dripping' in literal translation. In reality, it is a massive rock gallery cut by the Nabataeans

Fig. 92 – Qattar al-Aslaf.

in a place where water drips all year round. Right at the beginning of this gallery is the entrance to a small triclinium with the traditional three benches and a recess in the back wall, where betyls symbolising gods would have stood. Further on, a great many niches, betyls and inscriptions have been carved into the rock face. The most interesting of these is a niche containing a carved stone betyl bearing ... a cross of Lorraine with a Nabataean inscription alongside. Underneath this rock gallery, four water tanks have been cut out to collect water dripping into them from the rocks above. Even on the hottest of days, this spot remains pleasantly cool.

Let us return, however, to the path along the Wadi ed-Deir which heads towards the Monastery. If we look around from time to time, we can see the centre of Petra (dominated by the Royal Tombs) receding into the distance.

After passing through a small rock 'corridor', we come out onto a kind of rock terrace looking over an abyss from which we can see the urn standing atop ed-Deir for the first time. Attention should also be paid to the flat segment of rock to our right, which contains many visible entrances to its interior rooms, the walls of which have been carved with numerous crosses. This is called the 'Hermitage', although we do not know if this was in fact a place where Christian monks spent their lives alone. If they did, however, it must certainly have been the most picturesque hermitage in the whole of the Christian world at the time.

After the Hermitage, the path runs along the northern edge of a deep gorge towards the final steps we must climb to reach our goal. After several minutes of climbing, we find ourselves standing before the monumental façade of ed-Deir, the 'Monastery' **(Fig. 93)**.

Despite possessing the largest rock façade in all of Petra, ed-Deir does not make the same kind of bewildering impression as al-Khazneh, the Treasury. Perhaps this is because we can only admire this building in open space and not in the stunning location of a gorge surrounded by rocks. It could also

Fig. 93 – Ed-Deir (Monastery).

be because of the lack of rich relief decoration on its surface or its colour, which does not fit in with the rest of 'pink' Petra. Or maybe the architect, in an attempt to eclipse the earlier façade of the Treasury, added to ed-Deir to such an extent that it lost the wonderful proportions that Al-Khazneh relishes in.

Having said all of this, ed-Deir is still undoubtedly worthy of our admiration, above all for its impressive size; its two-storey façade is a massive 48.3 metres wide and nearly 47 metres high. The raw nature of ed-Deir's Nabataean style geometric decoration is also in stark contrast to the Hellenistic flourishes of the Treasury. Its positioning must also be highlighted. Cut out of honey-coloured sandstone, the façade stands alone on a wide plateau between peaks of rocks which boast impressive views in the directions of both the Wadi Araba and Mount Aaron. In order to fully appreciate the charm of the Monastery, it is best to come in the late afternoon, when it is lit by the rays of the dying sun.

The architect of ed-Deir undoubtedly drew his inspiration from the Treasury. However, it seems that he intended to turn his back on the Hellenistic splendour of his predecessors' work. Whilst the Monastery echoes the general structure of the building, the architect wanted to give its façade a more traditional, Nabataean character. At the same time, as was mentioned above, he wanted his 'Nabataean' façade to eclipse the foreign, Hellenistic one. He therefore developed it further by including additional pillars on both sides and on both floors.

Stylistically, the decoration of ed-Deir is closely linked to Nabataean tradition, although there are still classical elements present, such as the tholos, the Doric triglyph-metope frieze, the various types of gable (triangular, oval) and the decorated framing of the entrance and niches.

The façade is topped by a ten-metre high urn, which is positioned on a freestanding Nabataean capital. Not long ago, in the mid-1990s, it was possible to climb up to the top of the façade to see for yourself if the urn contained any treasure. However, the way is now closed off by a stone barrier and attempts to climb up are no longer welcomed by the park guards.

From the outside, ed-Deir is reminiscent of the Pharaoh's Treasury and the Corinthian Tomb, mainly because of the presence of a tholos situated between broken gables and the urn on top (**Fig. 94**). The main difference, however, is the total absence of figural decoration of the Monastery. Some researchers believe that figures were indeed once found in five niches cut into the façade of the building. It is not known, however, whether these were of human nature or if they were Nabataean stone betyls symbolising the gods. The latter seems far more probable. Another difference between ed-Deir and

Fig. 94 – The upper floor of the façade of ed-Deir.

the Treasury is the lack of freestanding portico columns. This raises the question as to why this is the case. The answer can be found by carefully studying the stone courtyard in front of the Monastery. If you do, it is possible to see bases on which columns forming porticos once stood on the northern and southern sides. The Urn Tomb was definitely the inspiration for these.

The interior of ed-Deir consists of a single, rectangular hall (measuring 11.25 by 12.1 metres) with two small benches (*biclinium*) to the sides and a niche cut into the back wall (about one metre above floor level), which has two rows of stairs leading up to it (one on either side) **(Fig. 95)**. A stone betyl probably once stood in this niche, whilst the crosses which are carved into it suggest that the building was later used in Byzantine times as a chapel. This would thus be the origin of its modern name.

There is one key question which we are currently unable to answer. Was ed-Deir used in the same way as the other façade tombs? Most researchers now believe that it was merely a temple which was dedicated to one of the first Nabataean leaders, perhaps Obodas I, who was laid to rest in Oboda. Here he may have been worshipped posthumously as a god and ritual feasts

Fig. 95 – Interior of ed-Deir.

in his honour could have been held in the *biclinium*. This is suggested by an inscription discovered here which is addressed to the god, Obodas. Perhaps ed-Deir also fulfilled the role of a cenotaph (a site which acts as a grave, but does not hold bodies of the deceased). But why did this temple-cenotaph appear so late on at the end of the 1st century CE, considering Obodas I died 150 to 200 years earlier. It remains a mystery.

Fig. 96 – Surroundings of ed-Deir.

The façade of ed-Deir appears very lonely, standing on its own amidst bare rock peaks **(Fig. 96)**. However, if you carefully observe its closest surroundings, the picture changes somewhat. In the past, as has been proven by research carried out by German archaeologists led by Manfred Lindner, the whole plateau would have looked quite different. Today, we can still see the remains of an altar (at the closest blocked rock entrance to the top of ed-Deir), numerous rock niches, cisterns collecting water, triclinia, rooms which were used as living quarters or storehouses and also a wide variety of other structures, the use of which has not been established for certain. All of this seems to confirm the theory that the whole plateau of ed-Deir was used by the Nabataeans as an open sanctuary or as an important cult place.

After a brief rest in front of ed-Deir, it is worth making your way to the numerous viewing platforms from which you can contemplate some wonderful vistas in the direction of the Wadi Araba or Mount Aaron. One of the best places to visit with this intention in mind is found directly opposite the façade of ed-Deir. On the way to this peak, it is worth looking into an enormous, rectangular, rock-cut room. Its back wall contains a niche which is cut in the form of an entrance with a double architectonic frame **(Fig. 97)**. Special attention should also be paid to the relief above the exterior pilasters, which presents a bust of the goddess Tyche/Fortuna.

Fig. 97 – The niche in the form of an entrance, opposite ed-Deir.

Looking south from the rock peak's viewpoint, we can see the summit of Mount Aaron and the albescent dome of its mosque towering over all the other peaks **(Fig. 98)**. To the west, if there is good visibility, we can make out the Negev Desert spreading out behind the Wadi Araba. The east, meanwhile, gives us a wonderful close-up view of the whole ed-Deir

Fig. 98 – View from the ed-Deir plateau towards Jabal Haroon (Mount Aaron).

complex. If you have more time at your disposal, you can ascend to further viewpoints which are very clearly marked by fluttering flags and advertising banners.

The trail ends in a descent to Petra along exactly the same route which we took when climbing upwards.

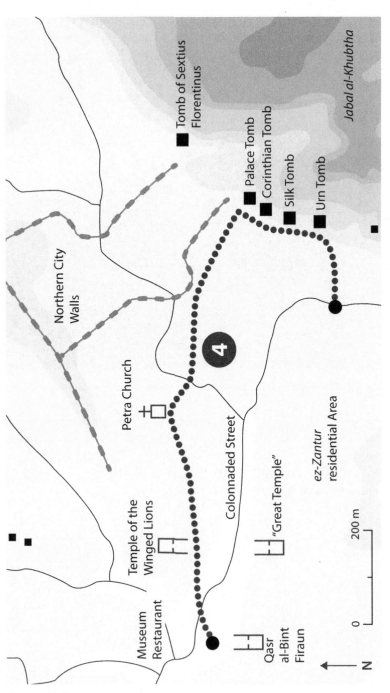

Fig. 99 – Trail No. 4.

The City Centre (North): The Temple of the Winged Lions – The Petra Church – The Royal Tombs (Fig. 99)

This trail leads us initially to two sacred complexes (a Nabataean temple and a Byzantine church) and then to the western slope of al-Khubtha, into which the façades of the Royal Tombs (the Urn Tomb, the Corinthian Tomb and the Palace Tomb) were cut. The whole journey should take no longer than approximately two hours and the trail is relatively easy.

The walk begins next to the museum and tourist centre in Petra. Heading first in the direction of Qasr al-Bint, we then turn to the left before the bridge and journey along the Wadi Musa to the remains of the Temple of the Winged Lions **(Fig. 100)**, which are visible to our left. This temple has been the subject of archaeological research for one of the longest periods of time and it is probably the Nabataean building which we know most about in Petra. American scholars have been carrying out excavations here for nearly 30 years, for much of that time led by Philip Hammond. Christopher A. Tuttle is, however, the man currently in charge. Over the course of the many years of research, many rooms which were used as residences or workshops have been uncovered adjacent to the temple itself. This has given us the first real opportunity to fully understand a whole Nabataean temple complex in

Fig. 100 – Temple of the Winged Lions with a Byzantine church in the background.

Petra. So, what did the complex of the Temple of the Winged Lions once look like?

From the side of the *cardo* (today the Colonnaded Street), across a bridge built over the Wadi Musa riverbed, one approached the monumental propylaea (gate), flanked on both sides by single porticos. Making use of alternating stairs and landings, one then moved towards the main building of the temple. The temple façade was formed by two imposing columns standing between antae (*distilos in antis*). Both the columns and the antae were topped by Corinthian capitals and the antae were additionally decorated by reliefs presenting human busts and torches amongst other things. Above this was a triglyph-metope frieze in the typical Nabataean form with circular metopes. The interior of the temple was formed of two parts, namely a vestibule and a square cella with 17.4 metre sides. A monumental entrance over four metres high led from the vestibule into the cella. The interior of the cella was stunningly decorated. The walls were adorned by half columns with niches between them, inside which stone betyls symbolising gods would have once been placed. In addition, rows of five freestanding columns ran along the western and eastern walls. Finally, in the northern part of the cella was an altar **(Fig. 101)**. It was a small raised platform (*motab*) surrounded by twelve columns with steps leading up both of its southern edges. The back part of the altar contained a small crypt, which would undoubtedly have been used to store the instruments needed in cult rituals. The whole interior was covered in plaster and fancifully painted. At first, the painted decoration

Fig. 101 – Interior of the Temple of the Winged Lions.

made use of Greco-Roman ideas, such as human figures, dolphins and vegetal or geometric motives. At the beginning of the 2nd century CE, however, when the temple was rebuilt, geometric ornamentation replaced the previous designs.

During investigation of the temple, the capitals that would have topped the columns surrounding the altar were discovered. These seem to have been unique, as they have not yet been found anywhere else. They were made of an upper and a lower part and took the form of circular stone drums. The lower part was decorated with typical Corinthian motives formed by acanthus leaves, whilst the upper was a unique combination of motives of flowers, pine-cones, palm branches interspersed with smaller branches and winged lions lying on beds of scattered acanthus leaves. It is from the decoration of precisely these capitals that the complex takes its name.

Over the course of the excavations conducted within the cella, archaeologists also came across a remarkably interesting example of a Nabataean stone idol **(Fig. 102)** with an inscription dedicating it to a goddess: *Hayyan, son of Nybat, dedicates this to the goddess …* Although we do not know to which goddess it is dedicated, thanks to the inscription we can be nearly certain that the temple was dedicated to a female deity. Researchers believe her to be one of the two most important female Nabataean goddesses, namely Allat or al-Uzza, who were later equated to the Egyptian Isis and the Greek Aphrodite respectively.

The cella was surrounded on three sides by a narrow corridor running along its walls. From the western corridor, it was possible to reach a small room which undoubtedly was the treasury of the temple. Amongst many other items discovered here, archaeologists have found a large amount of objects made of iron and bronze, amongst which a small figurine representing the Egyptian god, Serapis, is of particular interest.

Below the vestibule, archaeologists discovered over 1,000 marble pieces in all different stages of modelling, from raw to completely ready, which had been prepared to adorn the temple. Amongst the

Fig. 102 – Stone idol (betyl) found in the Temple of the Winged Lions (now in the Archaeological Museum of Amman).

pieces were three with a Nabataean inscription proclaiming the 37th year of King Aretas IV's rule. Is it therefore possible to determine that the temple was constructed before the 19th of April in 27 or 28 CE? Unfortunately, researchers are not completely convinced and prefer to place it in the 1st century BCE (which seems most probable) or the beginning of the 2nd century CE (although evidence suggesting this is almost certainly connected to its reconstruction).

As mentioned previously, aside from the building of the temple itself, a complex of rooms was also uncovered to the north-east (currently visible above the temple). These rooms were created somewhat later than the temple, although they were undoubtedly linked to it. To the north of the temple, there is also a large and nearly square courtyard (known as the 'Northern Courtyard'), which has stone benches on three of its sides. The entrance to the courtyard led from the eastern side through a gate flanked by double columns. Although archaeologists are not sure what the courtyard was exactly used for, it would seem that linking it to the Nabataean triclinia, where feasts in honour of the gods were held, would be the most logical solution.

The complex of the Temple of the Winged Lions was in active use until the 19th of May 363 CE, when a powerful earthquake utterly destroyed it. From later periods, only traces of short-term temporary usage of the building have been confirmed. These end completely with the next powerful earthquake, which the site suffered in 747.

Standing above the Temple of the Winged Lions, we can look across to the other side of the Wadi Musa for another sight of the Great Temple complex. If you pay particular attention to the completely differing natures of the structures, it should now be plain to see that the building across from us must have performed a secular rather than a sacred function.

To the east of the Temple of the Winged Lions are the ruins of a building which T. Bachmann described as the Royal Palace. Excavation work has not, however, been carried out here and we are thus unable to confirm or discard his theory.

About 150 metres to the east of the Temple of the Winged Lions, we come to remains from the Byzantine period of the largest Byzantine Church in Petra, discovered and researched in the first half of the 1990s by Zbigniew Fiema and others **(Fig. 103)**. The church is currently partially covered by a roof to protect the highly precious mosaics found within its interior. Over the course of archaeological research conducted here, it has been established that the church was built in the second half of the 5th century CE in a place which was previously a Nabataean living space, the beginnings of which date to the 1st century CE.

Fig. 103 – The Byzantine Church in Petra. In the background are the Blue Chapel and the North Ridge Church.

Today, we enter the complex from the south through a small entrance leading to a columned courtyard (*atrium*), from which it is possible to continue on to the interior of the basilica **(Fig. 104)**. The interior of the basilica measures 23.21 by 15.35 metres (a ratio of 3:2) and originally consisted of a wide central nave completed by an apse, two narrower aisles and a small rectangular rooms (*pastoforiae*) to the east. The aisles were divided from the

Fig. 104 – Atrium of the Byzantine Church in Petra.

main nave by two rows of columns. Many earlier Nabataean and Roman architectonic elements were used in the building of the basilica, coming no doubt from the buildings destroyed in 363 CE by the massive earthquake.

A large section of a mosaic floor (with measurements of 23.2 by 3.3 metres) was discovered in the western and central parts of the southern aisle (on the right). It presents animal figures (including lions, bears, deer, birds and fish) placed within rectangular and circular medallions and also personifications of the earth, the ocean and the four seasons. For this reason, the mosaic is known as the 'Master of the Four Seasons Mosaic' **(Fig. 105)**.

Fig. 105 – Part of the 'Master of the Four Seasons Mosaic'.

The first church was fronted by a vestibule, which was entered via a small courtyard. Opposite the church, on the other side of the courtyard, was a columned portico and a row of three rooms, the central one of which played the role of a baptistery (the place where believers were christened). The current entrance to the baptistery is now to be found in the north-eastern corner of the atrium. Once inside, we notice a large basin in the floor in the shape of a cross, which was used to christen adults through total immersion in water. There is also a small, circular vessel which would have been used to christen babies and small children. The baptistery would originally have been covered by a sort of canopy supported by four angular columns. The room before the baptistery has provided us with wonderfully preserved architectonic decoration from Nabataean times, which would once have formed the frame for a niche, perhaps with the image of a god. The decoration can now be admired in the new branch of the National Museum in Amman. A series of buildings were located to the north of the church which would have been used as living quarters. Two of these contained small passageways leading to the northern aisle of the basilica.

In the first half of the 6th century, the whole complex was completely rebuilt. The main change to the basilica involved the completion of the aisles, where the pastoforia was replaced with semi oval apses. In front of the apse of the main nave, a platform (presbytery) was also built and raised two levels. This was once separated off by a marble balustrade (a piece of which can now be viewed in the new branch of the National Museum in Amman). At the north-western end of the apse stood the pulpit. We do not know, however, where the altar would have been situated. At the back wall of the apse which closed off the central nave, stairs led up to a place where a bishop's throne was probably situated.

New mosaics also appeared along the whole length of the aisles and the floor of the central nave was laid with a parquet floor made of slate and marble using the *opus sectile* technique. In the northern aisle, an incredibly beautiful mosaic (measuring 22.6 by 3 metres) called the 'Master of Petra Mosaic' was created **(Fig. 106)**. It is composed of 84 circular medallions formed by vine branches, which are mainly filled by images of animals and birds, but also contain human figures (including a shepherd, camel-driver and a black man). The central row of medallions is mainly completed by images of vessels such as amphorae, craters and chalices. In the eastern part

Fig. 106 – Part of the 'Master of Petra Mosaic'.

Fig. 107 – The 'Master of the Chiaroscuro Mosaic'.

of the southern aisle, the small mosaic entitled the 'Master of the Chiaroscuro Mosaic' can be admired, which is formed of six circular medallions presenting animals **(Fig. 107)**. Two further mosaics were laid in the northern and southern apses, which took the form of chessboards with white and reddish-brown squares.

Within the interior of the basilica, a new pulpit was also constructed and most probably placed in the same place in which the previous one had stood. Outside, the vestibule was removed, thus connecting the basilica directly with the courtyard, which now took on the form of an atrium with a large water tank in the middle, surrounded by a two-storey columned portico.

Scrolls of papyrus also probably began to be stored in the north-western room of the complex at this time. Archaeologists discovered them while investigating the complex and, although they were largely destroyed, exhaustive conservation work has meant that they have provided us with much valuable information on the residents of Byzantine Petra. At the turn of the 6th and 7th centuries, the whole basilica complex was destroyed (probably by fire) and never rebuilt.

The discovery of the papyrus scrolls mentioned above was one of the greatest moments in the history of archaeological investigation into the Byzantine Church. 152 of them were found in total, some of which had writing on both sides and some only on one. The vast majority were written in Ancient Greek, the language used across the whole Byzantine Empire, although several texts made use of Latin borrowings. They were written by hand by scribes, who noted down the economic activity of the period. The scrolls concerned the ownership, acquisition and sale of land estates and other goods. They also described the signing of contracts and agreements, terms of lending, taxes, sales, division of inheritance, as well as weddings and deaths. The scrolls came from the years 528-592 CE and therefore from the times of Emperor Justinian and his successors. Many places of the time were mentioned within them, including Petra, which was termed *'Augustocolonia Antoniana Hadriana Metropolis (?) Provincia Palaestina Tertia Salutaris'*. Other contemporary churches are also mentioned, including some other churches in Petra which have not yet been discovered. By analysing the content of certain scrolls, it is possible to conclude with a high degree of certainty that the basilica which we have been describing functioned as a church dedicated to the Most Holy Virgin Mary ('Mary the Immaculate Virgin' to be precise). By comparing the texts with the results of archaeological research, we can also be almost certain that this was the basilica of the bishop.

Names which were very common among the highest social class such as the male 'Flavius' and female 'Kira' appeared in the texts. One of the most interesting scrolls of papyrus is dated to the 23rd May 537 and is unique in the whole of the Near East and Egypt. It describes a marital contract between Stephany, daughter of Patrophilos, and Theodoros, son of Obodianos. The Theodoros named seems to have been the owner of the majority of the papyrus stored at the basilica. He was most probably the archdeacon of the basilica, working directly for the Petraean bishop.

Fig. 108 – The Royal Tombs.

On leaving the church, we now turn in the direction of the mighty Royal Façade Tombs visible to the east **(Fig. 108)**. We first descend towards the wadi located to the east and then begin a gentle ascent up a path leading to two exceptional rock façades of the royal necropolis belonging to the Palace Tomb and the Corinthian Tomb.

Let us first approach the Palace Tomb, which lies to the left hand side. Its name derives from one of the first travellers to witness it, who it reminded of the Italian palaces with which he was already familiar. The façade of this tomb, one of the largest in Petra at 49 metres wide and 46 metres high, consists of three storeys **(Fig. 109)**. The two upper ones significantly differ in architectonic conception to the lowest one. The artists creating the tomb must have been of the same opinion, because they placed a flat, undecorated batten between the first and second floor, probably intending to mark a clear separation. The highest storey, which today practically no longer exists, had some of its design built onto it rather than being purely rock-cut. It was made up of several rows of undersized pilasters (eighteen in each row) with Nabataean capitals. These were placed precisely on top of the eighteen half columns of the middle floor below. Apart from the half columns (which were also completed by Nabataean heads), the middle floor contained six niches, where images of gods were probably once situated, perhaps in the form of rectangular betyls. The lower floor's main feature is that of four richly decorated entrances to four separate funerary chambers. Only the two central chambers are connected to each other by a narrow passageway.

Fig. 109 – The Palace Tomb.

The Palace Tomb must have belonged to the royal family of one of the last Nabataean kings of Petra, perhaps Rabbel II. This is shown by its positioning. If it had been built earlier, a site would have been found where it was not necessary to build onto the façade. However, since all of the possible locations had already been taken, it was necessary to cut it in another place and then execute the architectural conception by employing the technique of building onto the tomb itself.

The Corinthian Tomb, which lies just next to the Palace Tomb, also owes its name to one of the first travellers to see it, who mistakenly identified its columns and capitals as being of the Corinthian style **(Fig. 110)**. Forgetting the poor state into which it has now fallen, at first sight the Corinthian Tomb is reminiscent of the Pharaoh's Treasury. Indeed, if we look at the upper floor of the façade, we can make out a tholos flanked by two pavilions with broken pediments (the latter are identical to those of the Treasury). Looking further down, however, we can observe significant differences. Due to the placing of additional half columns at its sides, the lower floor is considerably wider than the upper. Furthermore, the trademark symmetry of Hellenistic monuments, which is visible above, is broken below by two additional entrance openings on the left-hand side. Each of the entrances (both the side ones and the main one in the centre) also has a different style of decoration. One might wonder what this is all about, yet the answer seems to be a simple one. We are dealing here with a splendid example of eclecticism, in this case a heady mixture of all

Fig. 110 – The Corinthian Tomb.

the different styles of Nabataean architecture. The artist working on this tomb copied designs from various other architectural constructions which he knew and used them to create a work he hoped would outshine them all. For certain, the design of the upper floor was directly copied from the Pharaoh's Treasury. The lower floor, on the other hand, is reminiscent of a widened Bab as-Siq Triclinium and the tomb façades cut into the rock walls of the Wadi Farasa. The question remains, however, as to which tomb was the prototype for the rest. Another question is still harder. For whom was this tomb intended? Again we can only draw a conclusion on the basis of architectonic decoration. In this case, the most suitable candidate is Malichus II, who died in 70 CE.

The interior of the Corinthian Tomb consists of four separate rooms. The largest, to which the central entrance leads, has measurements of 9 by 12 metres. On two of its walls, niches have been cut for the sarcophagi of the dead and it also has side entrances leading to the three remaining smaller chambers. Despite the fact that the Corinthian Tomb was undoubtedly hugely impressive at the time of its construction, it must be stated that the earlier Pharaoh's Treasury is by far its superior thanks to its more harmonious architectonic conception and its undoubtedly more scenic location.

Staying at the foot of al-Khubtha and moving a little further to the south of the Corinthian Tomb, we find ourselves in front of two Hegr type tombs

worthy of our attention, one of which (on the left when facing them) stands out in particular. This is the so-called Silk Tomb (**Fig. 111**). Although not particularly impressive in terms of size or architectonic decoration (mainly because of its badly preserved nature), it is the colour of the rock from which it is cut which catches our attention. A gorgeous, multi-coloured streak of sandstone gives the construction its unique appearance, which is reminiscent of the delicate colour of silk, the material after which the tomb is named. An analysis of its architectonic decoration allows us to place its creation in the second half of the 1st century CE. It was certainly not

Fig. 111 – The Silk Tomb.

the tomb of a monarch, but it most probably belonged to a high ranking official, perhaps even to a 'royal brother', the equivalent of a prime-minister today.

Moving further south we reach the stairs that lead us directly to the rock-cut courtyard, as well as two portico columns, in front of the Urn Tomb. A beautiful panorama of central Petra extends from it, with the mighty rock of Umm al-Biyara visible in the background on the left **(Fig. 112)**. Below the courtyard are two rows of underground chambers with arch ceilings, which the local Bedouins call the 'prison'. This could be a reflection of the function these buildings performed in the Byzantine period.

Fig. 112 – Panorama of the centre of Petra from the courtyard in front of the Urn Tomb.

The imposing façade of the Urn Tomb is over 26 metres high **(Fig. 113)**. From a distance, it creates an unusually light impression of harmonious composition and is reminiscent of the front of a Hellenistic temple. Four pillars, crowned by Nabataean capitals (of which the central two are half columns and the outer two are a combination of pilasters and quarter columns), support its highly elaborate entablature. Just over the columns, it is possible to discern four heads cut into the relief, probably of gods or of the Gorgons. Above this are four dwarf pilasters with Nabataean capitals, badly damaged by the hand of time. The pilasters hold up a triangular gable which is topped by a stone urn, which provides the tomb with its name. Three niches are visible within the façade between the half and quarter columns, the central one of which bears a relief slab with a bust which may present a

Fig. 113 – The Urn Tomb.

dead king (unfortunately, the head has not been preserved). Of interest is the fact that it was precisely in these niches that the deceased of the Urn Tomb were placed, one of them for certain being the leader for whom the tomb was constructed. Researchers suggest various possible candidates, including Obodas III and Malichus II. Nevertheless, it would appear, bearing in mind the prominent location of the tomb, the enormous amount of work which would have had to have been invested to create it (a large section of rock had to be moved) and in particular the very traditional, Nabataean style of its execution (despite the use of some later techniques for the architectonic decoration), that the ruler who was laid to rest here is the mighty Aretas IV, who died in 40 CE. Perhaps his two wives, Queen Huldu and Queen Shuqailat I, were placed in the two side niches. However, if Aretas IV was in fact laid to rest in the Pharaoh's Treasury (which has recently been suggested more and more often), then the Urn Tomb must naturally have had another leader as its occupant.

Three entrances lead inside the building, the central one of which is decorated in typical Nabataean style with pilasters, Nabataean capitals, a Doric triglyph-metope frieze and a triangular gable. The interior itself is a single chamber with measurements of 18.5 by 20.5 metres and a height of about ten metres **(Fig. 114)**. According to one theory, this chamber only performed the function of a triclinium. However, it is hard to find proof for this, since during the Byzantine period (about 446/447 CE), at the order of a bishop called Jason, the Urn Tomb was converted into a church and its exterior modified to fulfil the requirements of the Christian liturgy.

During the descent of the steps, it is possible to leave the route for a moment to take a path on the left towards the Tomb of Uneishu, which is described in Trail 1. It is not particularly clearly marked, but it would be very hard to get lost along it. After visiting the Tomb of Uneishu, we can wander between the various façades of the rock tombs for a moment, the majority of which must certainly have belonged to people who held a high position in the royal court.

Trail 4 ends at the Theatre. From here we can make our way back to the main Petra Tourist Centre in Wadi Musa.

Fig. 114 – Interior of the Urn Tomb.

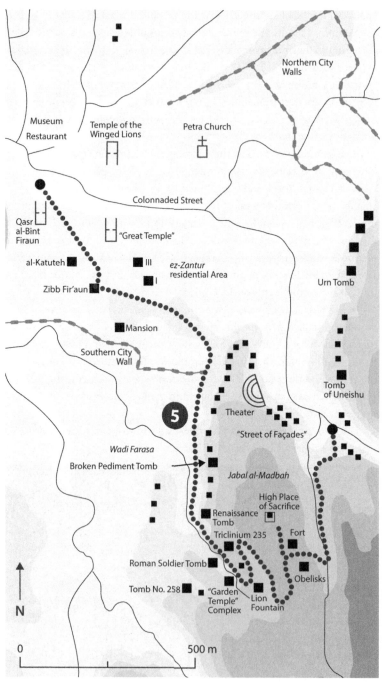

Fig. 115 – Trail No. 5.

TRAIL 5

The High Place of Sacrifice – The Wadi Farasa – Ez-Zantur (Fig. 115)

This route begins close to the Streets of Façades, where the Wadi Musa connects with the small, narrow valley of the Wadi Muhafir. It is precisely here that the Nabataean processional way leading to the peak of Jabal Madbah (meaning 'place of sacrifice' in Arabic) began. This is the most important cult site in Petra and is known as The High Place of Sacrifice. The whole trail should take about three hours to complete. It begins with a steep ascent of about half an hour and continues with a steep descent into the Wadi Farasa. The final part of the route is, however, considerably more straightforward.

Via rock-cut steps leading up steep corridors, we make our way to a sanctuary located about 200 metres above the city, following the same path Nabataean worshippers would once have taken. Special attention should be paid to the rock-cut corridors, the steps of which are sometimes barely visible **(Fig. 116)**. Every now and again it is worth turning around to admire beautiful views of the northern districts of Petra.

After climbing for about twenty minutes, the path turns abruptly to the right (west) to lead us to a place now occupied by Bedouin souvenir shop, where various paths cross one another. To the left (south) side, two graceful and mysterious Obelisks are carved out against a background of clear sky **(Fig. 117)**. Their heights reach 6.4 and 7 metres. Remarkably, they were created by clearing out the rock around them to create a level with a depth of over seven metres. Perhaps the rock removed from here was used to construct the nearby fort, but this would obviously imply that the fort and obelisks would have had to have been created at the same time. The function of these two obelisks has not yet been entirely agreed upon. They are most often seen as representations

Fig. 116 – The rock-cut steps.

Fig. 117 – One of the obelisks at the top of Jabal Madbah. Remains of the fort in the background.

symbolising two Nabataean gods, namely the god Dushara with either the goddess al-Uzza or Allat. However, others are of the opinion that both the obelisks and the high places themselves were inherited by the Nabataeans from their predecessors, the Edomites, who we know worshipped their gods amidst high rock.

Standing opposite the obelisks is a fort which has not yet been the subject of archaeological research. We therefore do not know if it was built by the Nabataeans, Romans, Byzantines or even Crusaders. According to another theory, it may have been a building connected in some way to the rituals being carried out at the peak of Jabal Madbah.

Behind the remains of the fort, at the very top of the elevation, the High Place of Sacrifice is to be found (**Fig. 118**). The walk towards it is best begun on a path running to the left of the fort. After a short climb, we find ourselves at the peak where the high place is located. It consists of a rock-cut courtyard (with measurements of 16 by 7 metres), two altars (one rectangular and one circular), a water tank and other installations which would have been useful during the performance of rituals. The courtyard is created on three sides by a typical Nabataean triclinium and in its centre there is a small platform, which could have been either a place were cult statues were situated (perhaps betyls) or a place where the priest conducted rituals.

Directly in front of the platform is the main altar, which is in the shape of a rectangle with measurements of 3 by 2 metres (**Fig. 119**). It is raised

Fig. 118 – *The High Place of Sacrifice.*

approximately one metre above the level of the courtyard and is surrounded on three sides by a kind of passageway, which could have been used in the performance of rituals. On the altar itself, there is an opening of about ten centimetres, into which it has been suggested that a cult betyl symbolising Dushara was placed.

Fig. 119 – *Rectangular altar of the High Place of Sacrifice.*

Next to the main altar, a second and somewhat smaller altar is located. This takes the form of a circle with a diameter of approximately one metre. It is very likely that libations were poured and animals sacrificed here. Some researchers also suggest the possibility of human sacrifice. Even today, shivers are sent down the spine when looking at the channels cut into the altar through which the blood of victims might have once flowed. In front of the altar is a water tank cut into stone which would have been used in cult rituals, perhaps to clean holy vessels. Not far from the courtyard, there is another water tank, which would probably also have been used in the ceremonies conducted here.

Those who have had enough of the sanguineous rituals of the High Place of Sacrifice can continue to a rock terrace located behind the courtyard, from which breathtaking views of the centre of ancient Petra (**Fig. 120**), as well as the rock elevations to its north, west and south (with Mount Aaron in the background), can be enjoyed. Descending to the final and somewhat smaller terrace, we find a path to our right which leads us back to the remains of the fort and the Bedouin shop mentioned above.

Fig. 120 – View from the summit of Jabal Madbah towards the centre of Petra.

Our route now continues along another Nabataean processional way, which once led to the peak from the south-west along the Wadi Farasa. We follow this down in the opposite direction to which it was used by Nabataean worshippers on their way to ritual ceremonies. Over the course of this route (down steps cut into the steep slope), we come across several Nabataean inscriptions and two rock relief compositions, the latter of

Fig. 121 – The 'Rock Mushroom'.

which are rarely encountered in Nabataean culture. The inscriptions can be seen about 100 metres down on the rock wall to our right.

After descending a little way towards the Wadi Farasa, we are confronted by a kind of 'rock mushroom' **(Fig. 121)**. At its 'stem', the first of the reliefs mentioned above is located.

It is a monument of about one-and-a-half metres in height which consists of a niche with a betyl cut into it, topped by a medallion bearing a depiction of a human bust **(Fig. 122)**. Archaeologists believe that this medallion and block relief was created in its entirety at the same time, most probably in the 1st century BCE. They also consider the betyl to be a traditional representation of the god, Dushara, whilst the medallion would present the god in his Greek form, Dionysus.

Fig. 122 – Rock-cut betyl and a medallion with the image of a human bust.

Fig. 123 – The Lion Monument.

Continuing on, we soon come to the second relief, which is named the Lion Monument **(Fig. 123)**. It is a five-metre-long figure of a lion, which is intelligently combined with a water channel to form a sort of fountain and water tank next to the processional way to the High Place of Sacrifice. The lion is often seen to be a representation of one of the Nabataean gods, perhaps the goddess al-Uzza. The rock bearing the relief could therefore have marked a site where ceremonies relating to a cult of the gods were performed. Or perhaps it was simply a resting place for pilgrims heading up the mountain, where they could have cooled themselves down using the water spouting out of the lion's mouth.

Opposite the lion relief, attention should also be paid to a rock-cut stone betyl, which would have either symbolised the god, Dushara, or have been a type of altar on which rituals were carried out during processions up to the summit.

The steeply descending steps then lead to the Garden Temple Complex **(Fig. 124)**. Situated in the upper part of the Wadi Farasa, this mysterious building was probably a temple, although we cannot rule out possible other uses. The name of the site derives from the small piece of land in front of its façade, which was considered to be a garden by the first travellers and researchers to visit Petra. The temple possesses a simple façade with two freestanding columns flanked by two pilasters, which together form a *portico in antis*. The columns and pilasters are topped by Nabataean capitals, which support an Ionic entablature devoid of a gable. The temple façade is

Fig. 124 – The Garden Temple Complex.

situated on a rock platform, which has some small steps leading up to it. On the platform itself, just before the façade, we can see the remains of a small cistern with two channels which transported water to and from the building. The interior of the temple consists of two rectangular rooms, one located behind the other.

Above the façade to the right (east), a five-metre deep water tank was built in rectangular form with measurements of 28 by 6 metres. This formed part of an important system supplying Petra with water from the spring of Ayn Brak, located to the south of the city. It was once possible to reach the water tank via steps to the left (west) of the temple façade. Behind the cistern are the remains of a room which was once covered by a curved roof. This room is clearly visible from the site of the previously mentioned 'rock mushroom' with the betyl of Dushara and medallion of Dionysus.

The Tomb of the Roman Soldier was cut out of the rock a little further along **(Fig. 125)**. With Triclinium 235 and the adjacent columned courtyard, it forms a well-integrated funerary complex, similar to that described on the inscription of the Turkmaniyya Tomb. Apart from its triangular gable and two half columns of differing size (flanked by angular pillars formed of pilasters and quarter columns, which were topped by Nabataean capitals), the Tomb of the Roman Soldier also contains three niches housing badly preserved human figures. The central statue presents a person dressed as a Roman soldier or legionary and gave the temple its name. To the right of

Fig. 125 – The Tomb of the Roman Soldier.

the tomb façade on a flat rock, we can observe a carved relief presenting a column crowned by a capital with two betyls on top.

The interior of the tomb consists of two rooms, of which the first (and larger) possesses three large recesses formed by curved arches in the back and right wall. There is also an additional small, rectangular niche cut into the back wall at ceiling level. To the left is the entrance to the smaller funerary chamber.

Opposite the façade of the Tomb of the Roman Soldier is a spacious triclinium, which was given the number 235 by Domaszewski (**Fig. 126**). Triclinium 235 stands out from other rock-cut buildings thanks to the fact that it boasts the finest interior of all the sites of Petra. It contains three broad stone benches and the walls above them were decorated with sculpted half columns, between which were recesses with oblong niches. The area surrounding the niches was additionally decorated with a simple pattern which formed a kind of frame. If we also take into account the fantastic reddish-silver colour of the rock (black was not the original colour, but was caused by the burning of a fire inside), then the whole structure would have looked very impressive. However, we must remember that the interior was probably plastered and painted over, an act which we would consider barbarism today.

An open courtyard, surrounded on three sides by portico columns, once stretched between the Tomb of the Roman Soldier and Triclinium 235 (**Fig. 127**). The whole of the complex has now been dated to the first half of the 1st

Fig. 126 – The interior of Triclinium No. 235.

century CE thanks to the most recent research conducted here by an international team of archaeologists under the leadership of Stephan G. Schmid.

Continuing along the Wadi Farasa, we can now take a brief detour to the charming little valley running alongside it, which is full of irises (which grow here in spring) and countless scattered fragments of Nabataean and Roman pottery. With this destination in mind, we turn left (south-west)

Fig. 127 – Colonnaded courtyard belonging to the complex of the Tomb of the Roman Soldier.

just after the complex of the Tomb of the Roman Soldier and enter the first valley situated on the left. Several interesting rock tombs were cut in this place. On the right (western) side, we can see the façade of Tomb No. 258 **(Fig. 128)**, whose appearance is reminiscent of that of the Tomb of the Roman Soldier. In fact, it only differs from it due to the lack of three niches housing human figures. Tomb 258, like the Tomb of the Roman Soldier, dates to the first half of the 1st century CE.

Fig. 128 – Tomb No. 258.

Deeper into the valley, one can find a further destroyed façade tomb, probably of the Hegr type, of which only fragments of the classical frame and side pilasters have survived. It is nevertheless worth looking inside the tomb to see its rock-cut niches decorated with architectonic details (rectangular pilasters completed by modest capitals).

On returning to the Wadi Farasa and continuing our path along its rock walls, after about 75 metres we come to the façade of the 'Renaissance Tomb' **(Fig. 129)**, which is carved into its right (eastern) side. It was so named by the author of an archaeological guidebook to Petra from the early 1970s (Iain Browning), who was reminded of the work of the Italian masters of the renaissance when studying the elegance of its façade. He was entirely justified in his appraisal. Although the tomb itself is not of particularly impressive dimensions, it nevertheless possesses very carefully selected and well-composed decorative motives. This tomb would have been constructed in the first quarter of the 2nd century CE, before the annexation of Petra by the Romans.

About fifty metres further to the north, also on the right (eastern) side, we come to the Broken Pediment Tomb, which dates to 40-70 CE **(Fig. 130)**. Despite its interestingly conceived gable, derived from the upper floor of the Treasury, it is not particularly impressive today. It is a sort of combination of the façade of the Tomb of the Roman Soldier with the broken gable known from other Petraean façades, which, in this case, does not produce a particularly good effect. This poor impression is perhaps exacerbated by the poor condition into which the façade has fallen.

Fig. 129 – The Renaissance Tomb.

Moving further north, to our right we can see further examples of façade tombs of the most varying styles, from small pylon tombs to elaborate façades of the Hegr type. Following a path along the ridge of Jabal Madbah,

Fig. 130 – The Broken Pediment Tomb.

we return to the Wadi Musa in the vicinity of the Royal Tombs. On the northern ridge of Jabal Madbah, we can see the remains of rock-cut houses and storage complexes, the walls of which are wonderfully decorated by the natural patterns of the sandstone itself **(Fig. 131)**.

Fig. 131 – One of the rooms on the northern slope of Jabal Madbah.

We now head towards a path which turns off to the left of Jabal Madbah and leads to a rectangular building (reconstructed and rebuilt by archaeologists), which we can see in the distance. It is located on the southern slope of the ez-Zantur elevation, where a residential area of Nabataean Petra once stood. It was exactly in this place (ez-Zantur IV) that a Swiss archaeological expedition led by Bernard Kolb, which had been working in Petra for many years, came across wall frescos reminiscent of the famous Pompeiian (Italy) ones within one of the residences.

Approaching ez-Zantur IV, we walk alongside a possible section of the southern city wall. Excavations which were conducted here about fifty years ago (supervised by Peter Parr) suggested that the southern 'fortifications' of Petra were located here. These would have started at the south-eastern end of the al-Habis elevation (directly in front of us) and continued along the northern edge of the Wadi Farasa all the way to the north-western slope of Jabal Madbah. Due to the lack of width to the wall, Parr believed that it was not a typical defensive structure and that it merely demarcated the boundary of the city. Today, certain researchers are even questioning his interpretation and go as far as suggesting that they were quite simply retaining walls for terraces, upon which houses and residences were once built in this part of Petra. In any case, it is difficult today to chart the precise course of the walls, although an observant eye will notice their remains in various places.

The Mansion was discovered by Swiss archaeologists on the site of ez-Zantur IV and its date of construction was placed in the 1st century CE. It is located in a place which affords a wonderful view of the southern districts of Petra **(Fig. 132)**. It had a surface area of about 1,100 square metres over two storeys and consisted of three main parts: the eastern section was for the servants and also contained guest rooms; the central and southern parts were the most decorative and guests would have been entertained here; finally, the western part was used for private purposes. The floors of the areas for entertaining and private purposes were partly laid with marble tiles using the *opus sectile* technique and two staircases located in the eastern and western parts of the Mansion led to the upper floor. The building was left in ruins after the great earthquake of 363 CE.

Fig. 132 – The Mansion (ez-Zantur IV).

The biggest sensation of the archaeological work conducted here was provided by the discovery of large preserved sections of wall decorated by frescos. The most interesting frescos are to be found in reconstructed Room 1 and present façades of unidentified buildings on a golden background. Although these could be mistaken for Pompeiian II style frescos (dating to around 80-20 BCE), they would have been created significantly later, more precisely in the 2nd century CE.

To the north of the Mansion, archaeologists have discovered the remains of a small chapel and altar. Work is still continuing on the Mansion site, with the aim of first protecting and reconstructing it, before eventually putting it on display to the public.

Continuing our journey, we can turn back on ourselves somewhat to observe the peak of the ez-Zantur elevation from the northern side. We also now have the opportunity to familiarise ourselves with the findings of Swiss investigation of the areas of ez-Zantur I and ez-Zantur III. In both cases, archaeologists dug up living quarters dating from the 1st century BCE to the 4th century CE **(Fig. 133)**. Typical Nabataean houses in the ez-Zantur district had dimensions of 30 by 30 metres and consisted of around fifteen rooms with open courtyards. They were divided into two parts, one private and one public. In some of the larger rooms, there were columns supporting a flat roof.

Fig. 133 – Nabataean house at ez-Zantur I.

Continuing through the uncovered houses, we can turn our attention to the remains of staircases leading to the upper floors and also to the beautiful views we have from here of the northern districts of Petra.

After visiting ez-Zantur III, we head further west in the direction of a clearly visible column standing on its own **(Fig. 134)**. This was named the 'Pharaoh's Column' (in Arabic "Zibb Firaun") by local Bedouins (and sometimes, in jest, the 'Pharaoh's Phallus'). It is made up of around fifteen stone drums, but its original significance has not yet been discovered. It was probably part of a monumental gate which led to one of the residences located on the ez-Zantur elevation, perhaps even to a royal palace.

At the Pharaoh's Column, the path continues north in the direction of Qasr al-Bint. We pass the al-Katuteh (meaning 'waste dump' in Arabic) elevation to the left (west), where it is possible to see the remains of an excavation carried out by Jordanian archaeologists in the 1980s. **(Fig. 135)** During their work, they uncovered the remains of many living quarters, but they were not, however, as spectacular as those which we have just visited in the ez-Zantur district.

The trail ends at Qasr al-Bint Firaun.

Fig. 134 – The Pharaoh's Column.

Fig. 135 – Al-Katuteh with Umm al-Biyara (left) and al-Habis (right) in the background.

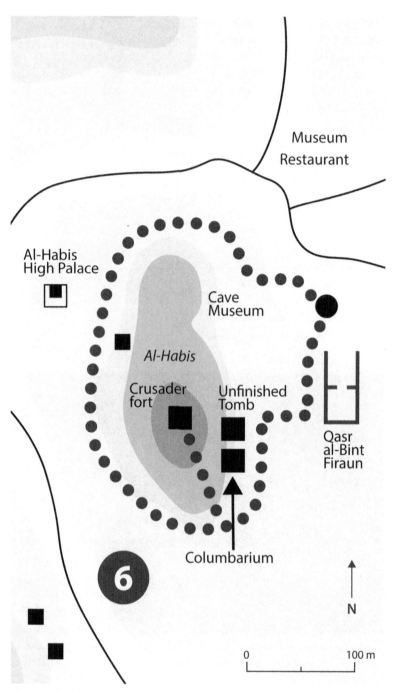

Museum
Restaurant

Al-Habis
High Palace

Cave
Museum

Al-Habis

Crusader
fort

Unfinished
Tomb

Qasr
al-Bint
Firaun

Columbarium

6

N

0   100 m

Fig. 136 – Trail No. 6.

TRAIL 6

Al-Habis (The Acropolis) (Fig. 136)

If you have some spare time, you can take one of the several short tourist trails of Petra which start from the area of the museum. One of these shorter options is a walk around the rock elevation of al-Habis, which lies to the west of the Qasr al-Bint temple. It should not take any longer than one or two hours, depending on the amount of time you would like to spend admiring the view at the summit. The only minor discomfort is the short but strenuous ascent to the top.

Ever since the times of J. L. Burckhardt, al-Habis has been called the Petraean Acropolis. This is not due to the function it performed (as is the case with the famous Athenian Acropolis), but due to its dominant position over the centre of the city **(Fig. 137)**.

Our walk around al-Habis begins at a 'rock' museum. The path we follow from here is cut out of the northern slope of the Acropolis and boasts views over the Wadi Siyyagh, which is a continuation of the Wadi Musa. We soon come to a rock courtyard (visible to the right) which was described as 'gar-

Fig. 137 – Al-Habis.

Fig. 138 – The al-Habis High Place.

den-like' by one of its researchers (A. B. W. Kennedy). Above its western wall and a rock-cut proto-Hegr tomb is a small area known as the al-Habis High Place **(Fig. 138)**. This spot, despite its relatively small size (3.7 by 4.9 metres), nevertheless possesses all the typical elements of high places, such as an altar, benches on three sides (triclinium) and a water tank, which was used during the performance of rituals. Behind the high place, looking further west, we can see a 'cut-out' vertical rock. This is the so-called quarry of the Wadi Siyyagh, from where blocks of rock were taken in order to construct many of the buildings in central Petra.

Opposite the al-Habis High Place looking east, there is a narrow rock path that you can take to the summit of the Acropolis. However, it is very narrow and has fallen out of use recently. For this reason, it is better to walk further to the southern slope of al-Habis, where a much more comfortable path to the top begins. To the right (when facing the summit), we should note a wonderfully preserved example of a simple Roman Temple tomb **(Fig. 139)**. Despite the presence of classical elements, its simple (or even raw) form makes it exceptional. The triangular gable here is supported by pillars made up of pilasters and quarter columns, which are completed by traditional Nabataean capitals. The simple frame of the entrance consists of pilasters holding up a double entablature on which a triangular gable (now invisible)

Fig. 139 – An example of the Roman Temple tomb type on the slope of al-Habis.

would once have stood. Through the use of stylistic analogies, we can date this tomb to the second half of the 1ˢᵗ century CE.

Continuing around the Acropolis, we soon come to its southern slope, from whence (as mentioned above) a steep but comfortable path leads to

Fig. 140 – Crusader Fort on the summit of al-Habis.

the summit. The only thing to have survived on the peak itself are the ruins of a small Crusader Fort **(Fig. 140)**, which was constructed around 1116 and deserted around 1188. This was part of the monitoring system of the strategic routes leading through Petra and its mother fortress was located nearby on the site of al-Wu'eira.

The ascent begins at a small courtyard, the remains of which adjoin the entrance to the path up. This path then takes us to the 'lower ward', via some reconstructed steps. Once here, we should head to its eastern side, from which we have a wonderful view of the expanse of central Petra. First of all, we have a highly detailed view of the Colonnaded Street leading to the temenos of the Qasr al-Bint temple. To the right, the Markets are located as well as the complex of the Great Temple **(Fig. 141)**. To the left, we can see the remains of the Temple of the Winged Lions and of the Byzantine churches. The background to all of these monuments is of course provided by the wonderful Royal Tombs on the slopes of al-Khubtha.

From the lower ward, we pass through the remains of a medieval gate to reach the 'upper ward', which is only a stone's throw from the peak of

Fig. 141 – View from al-Habis towards the Great Temple complex.

al-Habis. At the summit itself, there was once an observation tower. As was probably the case 900 years ago, the views from the Petraean Acropolis are breathtaking. Looking to the south, we see the Wadi Thugra **(Fig. 142)** leading towards Jabal Haroon and the Wadi Sabra. To the right of it, the mighty Umm al-Biyara proudly stands, whilst the Wadi Siyyagh runs off to the west. Looking north, we see the green belt of the Wadi Turkmaniyya disappearing

Fig. 142 – View from al-Habis towards Wadi Thugra and Wadi Sabra. In the foreground is the Crusader Fort.

Fig. 143 – The Columbarium.

into the distance. To its left the mountains of M'eisrah extend, on which we can see numerous façade tombs. Finally, looking to the east, we can once again contemplate the view of central Petra. Whilst admiring the archaeological complexes which have so far been created, it is easy to imagine the huge amount of work that still remains to be done by future archaeologists in order to uncover all of the remains of Petra which still lie buried under tonnes of sand.

After descending the Acropolis, we turn left onto a path leading along the eastern slope of al-Habis. After a short while, we come to two interesting rock-cut buildings. The first of these is called The Columbarium **(Fig. 143)**. Both its façade and rock-cut internal chamber are covered in small, square recesses with sides of 25 centimetres, which probably once contained urns with the ashes of the dead. Another theory has it that they once held doves, which were used in the cult of the goddess, Aphrodite/al-Uzza. Between the recesses, it is possible to see five considerably larger niches, which would once have contained images of gods in the form of betyls.

A little further along is the Unfinished Tomb **(Fig. 144)**, which was used to investigate the methods which the Nabataeans used to construct their rock façades. The first step was to pick a suitable rock face and then to prepare it in such a manner that a flat, vertical surface was obtained. Only after

Fig. 144 – The Unfinished Tomb.

this could the working of the stone begin, which was carried out from top to bottom. At the same time, work would also have been carried out under the chosen rock in the place where the funerary chamber, or interior (in the case of temples), was to be situated. The rock façade was then plastered and painted, as is attested by the remnants of stucco and paintings which have been preserved at the sites of several tombs. The colours of yellow, red and blue dominated in the paintings. Today, this kind of decoration could appear rather kitsch, but it must be remembered that even the wonderful Parthenon in Athens was gaudily coloured in the times of Pericles.

Leaving the Unfinished Tomb (which was probably intended to be a temple and not a tomb) unfinished, we finish our journey by descending down a path which emerges next to the temple of Qasr al-Bint.

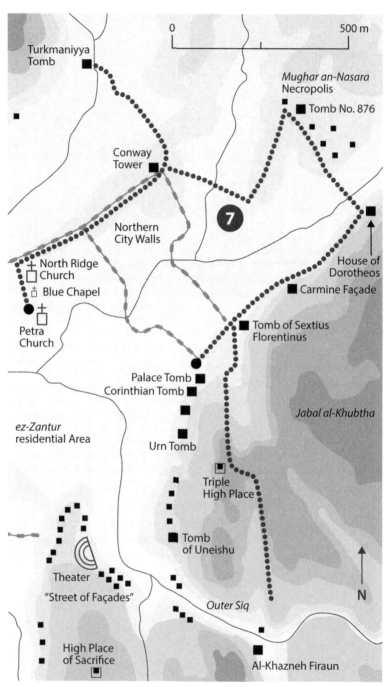

Turkmaniyya Tomb

Mughar an-Nasara Necropolis

Tomb No. 876

Conway Tower

0   500 m

7

Northern City Walls

House of Dorotheos

North Ridge Church

Blue Chapel

Petra Church

Carmine Façade

Tomb of Sextius Florentinus

Palace Tomb

Corinthian Tomb

ez-Zantur residential Area

Urn Tomb

Jabal al-Khubtha

Triple High Place

Tomb of Uneishu

N

Theater

"Street of Façades"

Outer Siq

High Place of Sacrifice

Al-Khazneh Firaun

Fig. 145 – Trail No. 7.

TRAIL 7

North Petra: Conway Tower – Mughar an-Nasara – Al-Khubtha (Fig. 145-146)

This trail is divided into two parts. The first is a fairly simple wander along the northern walls of Petra to the 'Conway Tower' (from which we can briefly descend to the Wadi Turkmaniyya) and the 'Christian District'. This section takes more or less two hours to complete. The only slightly uncomfortable sections are along little used paths between the Conway Tower and the Turkmaniyya Tomb and between the Conway Tower and the Christian District (Mughar an-Nasara). The second part is considerably more difficult, as it includes a fairly onerous ascent to the summit of al-Khubtha. It is, however, worth making the effort. Apart from the wonderful views of central Petra which this peak affords, we also have the chance to view the Pharaoh's Treasury from above. This section of Trail 7 should not take us longer than two and a half hours, but do not forget to carry water. The whole route ends close to the Royal Tombs.

Our walk begins next to the Petra Church (Trail 4) from where we head north. Just north of this complex, the remains of two further buildings from the Byzantine period were discovered. These buildings were the North Ridge Church (so named because of its location on the broad slopes of the Jabal Qabr Jumayan elevation (which run along the Wadi Turkmaniyya)) and a

Fig. 146 – The Northern Part of Petra.

small complex of rooms surrounding the 'Blue Chapel' (named after elements of architectonic decoration made of light-blue Egyptian granite found here).

The first site we come to is the Blue Chapel complex **(Fig. 147)**, which dates to the same period as that of the Most Holy Virgin Mary Basilica (the Petra Church), namely the second half of the 5th century CE. The complex was made up of several buildings, the most important of which was a three-aisled basilica of 12.6 by 11 metres, which acted as a private chapel. Its layout is reminiscent of the Petra Church as the large, central nave is also completed by an apse. The two smaller aisles (also completed by apses) were divided from the main nave by a double row of columns. It was precisely the scapes of these columns (taken from a previous, unidentified Nabataean building) which were made of the light-blue granite which gave the chapel its name. They were topped by typical Nabataean capitals, cut from white limestone, which when combined with the also white Ionic bases produced a stunning colour effect similar to that of the pinkish-red Petra. Over the course of investigation of the chapel, the remains of an altar, a pulpit (currently in the new branch of the National Museum of Amman) and an object resembling a throne were discovered. The latter could even have been sat upon by the Petraean bishop. The small size of the chapel, as well as the somewhat difficult access to it, have caused researchers to consider the theory that the Blue Chapel was not open to all believers, but that it was a private chapel within a larger residence, perhaps even that of the bishop of Petra himself.

Fig. 147 – The Blue Chapel.

Fig. 148 – The North Ridge Church.

The Blue Chapel was entered through a small vestibule which formed the centre of the whole complex. On leaving through the same vestibule, it was possible to enter the columned courtyard (atrium) to the east or to follow narrow steps to the north to the rooms which were used as living quarters.

Above the complex of the Blue Chapel is the North Ridge Church **(Fig. 148)**, built at the beginning of the 5th century CE above a Nabataean water tank (cistern). The church has the typical form of a three-aisled basilica with measurements of 18.1 by 13.5 metres. It was entered via a small, two-columned portico. The wide central nave was completed by an apse, whilst the narrower side aisles (which were divided from the central nave by a five-columned portico) were completed by small, rectangular pastoforia. The floor of nearly the whole basilica was made of rectangular sandstone blocks, with the exception of the presbytery, which was laid with marble tiles (*opus sectile*) or mosaics, which unfortunately have not survived to our times.

Continuing our journey, we now turn to the north of the North Ridge Church. A path is found here which runs along the remains of Petra's northern defensive walls **(Fig. 149)**. Peter Parr, who conducted research here in the 1960s, stated that they came from two different periods of the city. Nearer to the city itself is a series of walls from the Late Roman and Byzantine periods (3rd and 4th centuries CE). These run more or less from the Palace Tomb (visible in the distance) in a north-westerly direction through the Wadi Mataha (where a gate would have stood) to the peak of Jabal Qabr Jumayan, where we now find ourselves. A little further to the north are fortifications from

Fig. 149 – The Northern Walls of Petra with Umm al-Biyara in the background.

an earlier period, when the state of Nabataea still existed. These begin at the Tomb of Sextius Florentinus and run all the way to the Conway Tower, which is the place to which we are now heading. The shrinking of the size of the city, which is demonstrated by the repositioning of the city walls, was most probably caused by the decreasing importance of the city and with it Petra's gradual decline.

Continuing further north along the city walls, we soon come to the section which is best preserved. It was in this place that Peter Parr and then Philip Hammond carried out their excavations. The uncovered section of the walls is about two metres in breadth and it is also possible to see the remains of rectangular towers contained within it.

Finally, we come to the Conway Tower (which is preceded by other sections of a defensive wall uncovered by archaeologists, at the start of which we can observe the remains of a rectangular tower). Known to the Bedouins of Petra as "al-Mudawwara" (the 'Circle'), the Conway Tower is a near-circular construction with a diameter of about 25 metres **(Fig. 150)**. It is surrounded by four-metre thick stone walls and to its west and south are adjoining city fortifications. The Conway Tower is now considered to have been the most northerly part of the Petraean defensive system and it would have been constructed in the city's heyday. It was, however, previously misidentified as a high place.

Standing at the top of the tower, we can admire views of the northern perimeter of Petra. To the east, the mighty elevation of al-Khubtha dominates with the Royal Tombs cut into its slope standing alongside rock houses and channels carrying water (further to the north). The Wadi Mataha and the Wadi Umm Sayhun extend towards the north, between which the elevation of Mughar an-Nasara lies, its façade tombs already visible from here. To the west of the Conway Tower is one of Petra's most beautiful valleys, the Wadi Turkmaniyya/Abu Olleqa, which today is still full of gardens and green, blooming oleanders. It is here that the next important stop of the trail

Fig. 150 – The Conway Tower.

is to be found in the shape of the Turkmaniyya Tomb **(Fig. 151)**. It is located a little to the north-west of the Conway Tower and can be reached via one of the paths leading downhill in the direction of the Wadi Turkmaniyya.

The badly preserved Turkmaniyya Tomb was cut in the elaborate Hegr style and dates to between 40 and 70 CE. It is on this tomb that the longest (and probably most important) Nabataean inscription discovered in Petra so far was found. Amongst other things, it describes a complete Nabataean funerary complex:

"This tomb and the large and small chambers inside, and the graves made as loculi and the courtyard in front of the tomb, and the porticos and the dwelling places within it, and the gardens and the triclinium, the water cisterns, the terrace and the walls, and the remainder of the whole property which is in these places, is the consecrated and inviolable property of Dushares, the God of our Lord..."

Fig. 151 – The Turkmaniyya Tomb.

The interesting aspect of this description is that the tomb was part of a complex which was inhabited by living people, something which has not been confirmed by any other inscription, ancient account or archaeological investigation. Despite the fact that none of the constructions mentioned in the description have been discovered in the vicinity of the Turkmaniyya Tomb (no standard archaeological investigation has yet been carried out here), the inscription represents a kind of ancient guide to the type of complex found around other tombs, such as the Tomb of Uneishu or others lying within the Wadi Farasa.

The easterly peak of the mountains of M'eisrah, which is called Jabal M'eisrah as-Shargi, rises above the Turkmaniyya Tomb and another high place can be found here. This mountain divides two separate valleys, along which many tens of hugely varying rock tombs can be seen. After becoming acquainted with the Turkmaniyya Tomb, we return towards the Conway Tower before turning to the north, where a group of rock elevations termed Mughar an-Nasara are located **(Fig. 152)**. These possess a large number of very different types of façade tombs.

Firstly, we have to turn off onto one of the poorly demarcated paths leading east, in the direction of the Wadi Mataha and the Wadi Umm Sayhun (which contains visible remains of the northern walls of Petra). In the place where the two wadis meet, we hit a clear path which leads from the base of the Palace Tomb to Mughar an-Nasara. Whilst the section leading towards the Palace Tomb is very sandy, the section leading north is largely cut out

Fig. 152 – Mughar an-Nasara.

of the rock and forms a part of the former Nabataean road (caravan route) to the north in the direction of the Negev Desert and later the Mediterranean Sea.

Mughar an-Nasara is often referred to as the 'Christian District' due to the numerous crosses cut into its caves and tombs. The name of the elevation translates from the Arabic as the "Cave of the Nazarenes". This title of the people of Nazareth, a place connected with the life of Christ, was once used in these territories as a general term for Christian Arabs. People who had adopted the name in this sense may well have therefore taken this area into their possession. Whether this be true or not, the area was certainly the northern necropolis of Petra in Nabataean times, which extended along the road leading out of the city in the direction of the Negev Desert.

In the Mughar an-Nasara region, two of the many rock-cut tombs are worthy of special consideration. They are found to the right of the previously mentioned Nabataean rock-cut road and stand out very clearly thanks to their 'honey-coloured', wonderfully preserved façades (**Fig. 153**). Due to their colour, they look particularly stunning in the afternoon in the light of

Fig. 153 – Tomb No. 876 (left) with the triclinium (right).

the dying sun. To be accurate, however, they are not both tombs. One is a tomb, but the other is a triclinium and they both form part of a large funerary complex, the defining feature of which is a large courtyard made up of various installations such as altars, channels and water collecting cisterns. Together, the complex fits the description of the Turkmaniyya inscription very well.

The most interesting part of the complex is the façade of Tomb 876 itself, which is of the Hegr type with a double frame entrance. Four dwarf pilasters can be seen above it, between which the reliefs of two Medusa heads and a frieze presenting armaments (mainly shields) have been sculpted. This depiction of armaments is unique in Nabataean art. Inside the tomb, all three walls contain niches where the dead would once have been placed. The façade belonging to the triclinium is similarly constructed in typical Hegr style with a double frame entrance. This one, however, lacks relief decoration and undersized pillars. Inside on the left is a bench (*kline*) on which ritual meals would have been taken. The remaining two were probably removed and replaced by niches, which the dead would later have been placed in.

Just next to the funerary complex, on the other side of the rock-cut road (about two to three metres wide at this section), we can see the remains of a rock-cut complex surrounding a courtyard, which is considered to have once been a sort of caravanserai. It was, however, probably also a funerary complex and the remains of architectonic decoration on the northern side of the courtyard, reminiscent of Nabataean tomb façades, support this theory.

About fifty metres further to our east is a very interesting, but badly destroyed façade tomb. It contains a richly decorated entrance and four pilasters holding up a … non-existent entablature. This façade halts abruptly, as if the artist stopped work halfway through. The explanation of the missing entablature is, however, very simple. As was the case with the Palace Tomb, it was probably built onto rather than cut out of the rock. The entablature would thus have been taken down later and used for other purposes. Maybe one of the local crusader towers or Bedouin farmhouses hides the remains of this tomb entablature from Mughar an-Nasara. We do not know.

If you are not pushed for time, it is pleasant to walk at your leisure for a longer period of time through the northern necropolis of Petra.

We next make our way further east towards the north-western slope of the mighty elevation of al-Khubtha. Two rows of rock-cut 'windows' (one underneath the other) can be seen on it, underneath a channel which transports water to the centre of Petra. This is the next stop on this trail, the House of Dorotheos **(Fig. 154)**.

Fig. 154 – The House of Dorotheos.

On the steep, north-western slopes of al-Khubtha, many houses, individual rooms, votive niches and water channels and tanks have been cut into the stone. The most interesting collection of these elements is the mysterious complex which is known as the House of Dorotheos. These are probably the remains of a private living complex. Rock-cut steps lead to a small courtyard, next to which a spacious triclinium (11.8 by 11.4 metres) is found. Three entrances situated below three windows lead to the interior. Apart from three stone benches, two Greek inscriptions bearing the name of Dorotheos (perhaps the owner of the whole complex) were discovered inside. Although it seems, based on the inscription, that the triclinium was used in a domestic way (perhaps to consume meals or entertain guests), this does not rule out the possibility that it was also used as a place of feasting in honour of the dead.On the rock above the House of Dorotheos, a clearly cut channel can be seen. Water would have flowed through here from the cisterns of al-Birka to the centre of Petra. The positioning of the channel is highly impressive and gives us an idea of the immense skill which the Nabataean constructors must have possessed in order to execute this hydrotechnical system, which was so vitally important to the city.

After visiting the House of Dorotheos, we turn to the south. We pass further rooms (including a small tomb, a triclinium and votive niches) before coming to the Carmine Façade **(Fig. 155)**. The name originates from the intensely red sandstone out of which it is cut and it is a most beautiful example of a façade with a developed gable style. It consists of two pilasters (topped

Fig. 155 – The Carmine Façade.

by Nabataean capitals) which support a double Ionic and Doric entablature, above which a triangular gable rises. The dwarf pilasters which separate the Ionic and Doric entablatures are also worthy of note and the whole façade should most probably be dated to the 1st century CE. For unknown reasons, no funerary chamber was built. We do not know if this was the intention (in which case the façade could be seen as a kind of cenotaph) or if there was simply not enough time or money to finish it.

Several minutes further along the western slope of al-Khubtha, we come to the tomb situated the furthest north in the royal necropolis. This is the Tomb of Sextius Florentinus **(Fig. 156)**, a Roman governor of the province of Arabia, who died in 129 CE. Despite the very badly preserved nature of the façade, it is one of the richest and most refined in terms of architectonic decoration in all of Petra. It possesses nearly everything: a double frame entrance, half columns and pilasters with Nabataean capitals, semicircular and triangular gables, vegetal ornaments, busts probably presenting one of the gods or the Gorgons/Medusa and the figure of an eagle. All of this is combined to create a masterfully harmonious whole, which still makes a hugely striking impression today. Inside the individual chambers of the tomb, there are niches on the back and one of the sidewalls. Sarcophagi with the bodies of the dead were placed here. Thanks to a Latin inscription with the name of Sextius Florentinus, found on the entablature above the entrance to the tomb, this is the only precisely dated façade in the whole of Petra.

Fig. 156 – The Tomb of Sextius Florentinus.

Several minutes further south, we come to the beginning of an ancient Nabataean processional way leading to the top of al-Khubtha **(Fig. 157)**. It lies almost exactly between the Tomb of Sextius Florentinus and the Palace Tomb (Trail 4) and is currently the simplest way to reach the summit. There

Fig. 157 – The Nabataean processional way to the summit of al-Khubtha.

are two other paths, which begin at the Urn Tomb and the Pharaoh's Treasury, but the latter is off limits at present.

We begin the ascent on steps located behind a reconstructed wooden gateway. After about ten to fifteen minutes, we come to the first terrace. If we turn around here, we can enjoy the beautiful views that give us our first sight of the 'Christian District" (Mughar an-Nasara). A moment later, we come to a place with a panorama of Petra's city centre.

In front of us there is a further set of steps that continue the climb. On approaching these, let us pay attention to the superstructure visible to our right, which is the highest part of the Palace Tomb façade. Also to our right, an observant eye will be able to see the remains of a Nabataean inscription situated next to a small cult niche. The final ascent then begins, which leads us to the peak of al-Khubtha.

Right at the end of the steps, we can see three small high places which together are termed the Triple High Place **(Fig. 158)**. These are small, rock-cut courtyards (sometimes with small altars and water tanks), which are located on individual rock platforms.

Fig. 158 – One part of the Triple High Place on the summit of al-Khubtha.

All of them are situated in a manner which would have kept the centre of Petra and its most important temples (including Qasr al-Bint Firaun) in clear view during ritual proceedings. There are also great views from here in almost all directions. To the south, the Jabal Madbah High Place of Sacrifice and the Theatre are both visible **(Fig. 159)**.

Fig. 159 – View from al-Khubtha to the south.

Moving to the south-east of the first two platforms (the third is located approximately fifty metres east of them), we come to the remains of a large water tank, which is closed off to the north by a small dam built of regularly worked stones **(Fig. 160)**. In Nabataean times, this would have been covered by rock slabs, which can be attested by the remains of supports which once

Fig. 160 – Water reservoir with a small dam.

Fig. 161 – Stone altar with a rectangular betyl.

would have held up a ceiling. Below and to the north, the Wadi Khubtha begins on its path towards the Tomb of Sextius Florentinus.

Fig. 162 – Al-Khazneh Firaun. View from al-Khubtha.

Looking to the other (northern) side, we see a small wadi which gently descends towards distant rocks. At the beginning of this valley, on the right, a mysterious stone altar is cut into the rock, to which a partly preserved set of steps leads (**Fig. 161**). At the back of its small courtyard, a rectangular betyl was cut, which takes up the whole of the back wall. We cannot yet be sure, however, as to whether this was a site of feasting or a place where additional rituals connected to the high places were carried out.

After several minutes of descent into the wadi mentioned above, we come to a place from whence we are able to once again admire the Pharaoh's Treasury, this time looking onto it from above. From here we

Fig. 163 – The return path from al-Khubtha.

can descend to a place which nearly directly faces the façade of the Treasury **(Fig. 162)**, although great care must be taken here, since there is no kind of barrier to protect you from falling into the valley below. From this perspective, it is possible to appreciate the massive size of this beautiful building in comparison to the seemingly miniature people at its base.

After taking in the view of the Pharaoh's Treasury, we return on exactly the same path **(Fig. 163)** which we took previously all the way to its exit between the Palace Tomb and the Tomb of Sextius Florentinus.

The trail ends at the Palace Tomb.

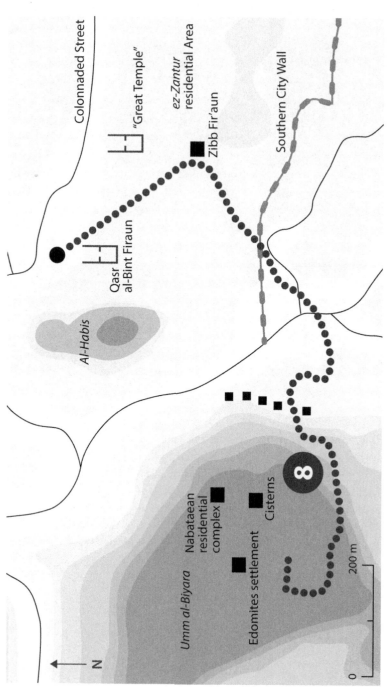

Fig. 164 – Trail No. 8.

TRAIL 8

Umm al-Biyara (Fig. 164)

This trail is for the somewhat more experienced tourist. Umm al-Biyara is a mighty rock rising to the south-west of Petra and a journey to its peak will afford us unforgettable views of both Petra and its surrounding area. However, in order to reach its peak, it is necessary to complete an extremely steep ascent lasting approximately one hour and also to make sure you do not stray from the path leading to the summit. The whole expedition should take no longer than about four hours. It is absolutely essential to pack sufficient supplies, especially water (a bare minimum of 1.5 litres per person), since there is no possibility of replenishing your stocks along the way.

We begin the trail next to Qasr al-Bint Firaun in central Petra, from whence we travel south in the direction of the Pharaoh's Column (visible in the distance). We then head downhill in the direction of the extensive Wadi Thugra, the western wall of which is created by the mighty Umm al-Biyara rock **(Fig. 165)**. Attention should be paid to the numerous façade tombs

Fig. 165 – Umm al-Biyara.

Fig. 166 – The preserved remains of a gate (on the right).

which are cut into its side. Here you can see arch tombs, which are rarely encountered in Petra.

On entering a small wadi located opposite the largest façade (of the Hegr type, badly damaged) cut into the face of Umm al-Biyara, we turn to the right and head in the direction of a small tree which can be seen up and to the left behind the façade. Some steps are visible near the tree and it is up these that we begin our journey to the peak. As early as the first terrace, which we reach after very little time, we are able to enjoy some wonderful views, particularly in the direction of ez-Zantur. We then head north and, after crossing a restored bridge, we find ourselves standing in front of a further set of steps. The preserved remains of a gate can be seen here, which once would have closed off access to the summit **(Fig. 166)**.

Fig. 167 – Rock passage leading to the summit of Umm al-Biyara.

Continuing our climb, we come after a moment to a wide rock passage, which seems to be closed off by a rock wall **(Fig. 167)**. This is, however, merely an illusion. When we reach its end, two narrow rock-cut corridors appear on either side of the wide passage, which lead off at an angle of 180 degrees. The better preserved one is located to the south (left, when facing the rock) and we continue our journey along it.

After a short while, we find ourselves above the passage (with beautiful views down), where another set of steps begins **(Fig. 168)**. These lead us without any further difficulties to the summit of Umm al-Biyara in about thirty to forty

Fig. 168 – Steps leading to the summit of Umm al-Biyara.

Fig. 169 – One of the water tanks (cistern) at the top of Umm al-Biyara.

minutes. Making our laborious way up the steps, there will be plenty of views to whet our appetite for what awaits us at the top.

In Arabic, the name Umm al-Biyara means 'Mother of Cisterns' and this originates from the large amount of water tanks (cisterns) which are cut into its peak (**Fig. 169**). Indeed, when we stand upon its wide plateau, the first thing that leaps to our attention are the still functioning little channels of water carved into the surface of the rock. These channels deliver falling precipitation to a series of cisterns, the upper openings to which cover practically the entire summit. Whilst walking around the peak of Umm al-Biyara, special care must be taken to avoid falling into them.

At the centre of the elevation, we can see the remnants of a British excavation led here by Crystal-M. Bennet in the 1960s. They found the remains of a settlement of Edomites, which was occupied in the Iron Age (**Fig. 170**).

Fig. 170 – The remains of a settlement of Edomites.

Fig. 171 – Part of the Nabataean residential complex (palace?) on the top of Umm al-Biyara.

The archaeologists also paid special attention to remains found to the eastern side of the elevation, which they described at the time as either a former Nabataean high place or sanctuary. In 2010, a new excavation was started here led by archaeologists Piotr Bienkowski and Stephan G. Schmid within the framework of the International Umm al-Biyarah Project (IUBP). During their investigation, they discovered that the remains found here were not of a temple, but rather those of an extensive residential complex **(Fig. 171)**. It has even been suggested that they may have been part of a royal palace, built using the palaces of Herod the Great in Masada and Jericho as prototypes. These were both places which were very difficult to access, but which guaranteed the safety of the king. Thus far, the remains of a bathhouse, as well as numerous fragments of marble statues (including that of a boy with a jug of water) have been discovered **(Fig. 172)**.

To the east of the summit are the remains of a building which was probably an observation tower. Umm al-Biyara was, of course, absolutely perfect for this purpose. Looking in any direction, we are met by enchanting, rolling views. Looking to the east, we see the expansive Wadi Musa with

Fig. 172 – Fragment of an architectural decoration of the residential complex.

the remains of Petra and the Royal Tombs cut into the side of al-Khubtha **(Fig. 173)**.

Looking north and west, we see the mighty rock summits heading out into the Wadi Araba and the Negev Desert. The most important element of the

Fig. 173 – View from Umm al-Biyara towards the centre of Petra.

Fig. 174 – View from Umm al-Biyara towards Jabal Haroon.

panorama, however, is the majestically rising Jabal Haroon, with the white dome of its mosque visible at its summit **(Fig. 174)**.

After covering the whole peak of the 'Mother of Cisterns', we return to the steps we have just ascended and head down them following exactly the same route which we followed earlier in reverse.

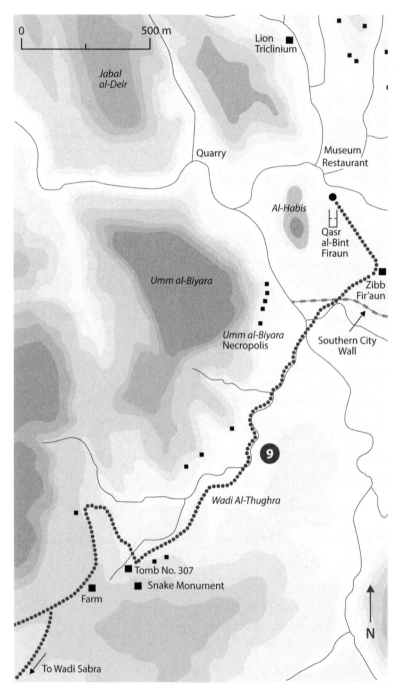

Fig. 175 – Trail No. 9.

The Wadi Sabra (Fig. 175)

A visit to the Wadi Sabra, which is situated about seven or eight kilometres from the centre of Petra, is only for hardy, experienced travellers and best done as part of a group. This is not only due to the length of time it will take (about six or seven hours), but also because of the need for an excellent sense of direction, as it is very easy to stray from the path.

Our goal is an expansive valley, where the remains of a small, rock-cut Nabataean theatre and the remains of several buildings (including a temple) are to be found, situated upon what was once a small 'acropolis'. This probably once constituted the centre of a small settlement lying to the south of Petra.

Over the course of the trip, you are unlikely to meet any other tourists, but you will certainly be able to delight in some beautiful views of the southern surroundings of Petra. It is essential to have good walking boots (preferably reaching up to the ankles) with hard, Vibram rubber soles, as while walking along sandy and rocky trails it is very easy to injure yourself. It is also essential to take a mobile phone and a suitable amount of supplies (an absolute minimum of three litres of water), as there is no possibility of replenishing them on the route.

It should also be remembered that it is always possible to hire a guide (prices range between twenty to fifty Jordanian dinars), which is expensive, but ensures that you will not stray from the route or follow unnecessary paths. The local Bedouins know the terrain like the back of their own hand.

The trail begins next to the Qasr al-Bint Firaun temple in the centre of Petra. We head south from here, in the same manner as we did on Trail 8. After passing the Pharaoh's Column and descending, we take a wide, sandy road running south along the Wadi Thugra, which is used by off-road vehicles. A gentle climb then begins, which should take about forty minutes to an hour. From time to time, we will see Nabataean tomb façades of various styles. Keeping to the main road at all times, with the mighty rocks of Umm al-Biyara and then Jabal al-Quray to our right, we head towards some brightly-coloured stone hills which we can see in the distance, where tombs of the Petraean southern necropolis were cut. Unfortunately, some of them are currently being used by Bedouins for both economic and dwelling purposes.

Two of these tombs are exceptional. The first is the freestanding Pylon Tomb 307 **(Fig. 176)**, which is visible from a distance. It takes the form

Fig. 176 – Pylon Tomb No. 307.

Fig. 177 – The Snake Monument.

of a tower (similar to what we saw in Bab as-Siq) standing on a multi-level platform. Particular attention should be paid to the very well-preserved double row of crowstep frieze which adorns it.

After reaching the rock from which it rises, we find ourselves in front of the buildings of a Bedouin family. Here, we should look upwards and to the left. Above the eye-catching Tomb 303, which is rock-cut on three sides, we will see the so-called Snake Monument for the first time, which presents a serpent coiled three times on a rock cube with sides of two metres (**Fig. 177**). It is believed that this monument was the symbolic guardian of the southern necropolis, or perhaps even of the whole southern border of the city.

From here, it is about a ten minute climb to a broad plateau. Looking back, we have excellent views of the suburbs of Petra (the Royal Tombs can even be seen in the distance) and just before us Tomb 307, Tomb 303 and the Snake Monument (to the right). Returning to the route, we soon come to the 'farm', an enclosed, overgrown area containing all manner of plants. Continuing south, just after the farm, we come to another wide plateau. This is a critical juncture on our route, as it is very easy to lose your way here (**Fig. 178**).

Our target is situated between two high rock peaks visible in the

Fig. 178 – Path from the 'farm' to the Wadi Sabra.

distance. The first of them (in front and to our right) is a wide rock ridge, while the other (to its left) is a double rock peak. Between them is a sheer, conical rock towards which we should now head, preferably taking a route along the broad Wadi Maqatal. The rock 'cone' should be passed to its right (keeping it to our left-hand side). Behind it, the wadi turns left (east) and soon leads to a place with a wonderful view of the Wadi Sabra (**Fig. 179**). The main feature of this wadi is a small oasis in the centre of the valley, the point to which we are heading.

Several paths lead down into the Wadi Sabra. The easiest of these is along the western ridge (on the right). It is also possible to continue the trip on a path along the eastern ridge of the wadi all the way to the remains of an observation tower situated above the valley itself. However, the only way down from here to the Wadi Sabra is a rock slope, difficult to complete even for the most experience explorers.

After descending to the bottom of the valley, we continue our journey along the wadi (which is winding south) to the remains of a small theatre situated on the left (east) rock slope of Jabal al-Jathum, just before the green

Fig. 179 – The Wadi Sabra.

oasis. It is also possible to see a great deal of stone rubble just before the theatre, also to the left. It is probable that some houses were built here by the erstwhile residents of the valley.

Within the Wadi Sabra, there are architectural remains dating to the Hellenistic and Roman periods. These were discovered in 1828 by Leon de Laborde, the famous French traveller and orientalist. During his short stay, he sketched a cursory map of the valley and made a drawing of the remains of the theatre standing here. Short descriptions of the valley were also made by R E. Brünnow and A. von Domaszewski (1904) and later A. Kammerer (1928). The first surface research of the area of the Wadi Sabra was carried out in the 1930s by Nelson Glueck, who confirmed the dating of the principal remains to the period between the 2nd century BCE and the 2nd century CE.

Further research was only carried sporadically between 1963 and 1982 and then again in 1990 by the Naturhistorische Gesellschaft Nürnberg within the framework of the Sabra Project led by Manfred Lindner. This was largely surface research, but as a result information was verified concerning the main complexes located within the wadi: the theatre, the small 'acropolis' (supporting the remains of a temple), the advanced hydrotechnical system which collected and transferred water, the residences and the necropolis. A quarry was also discovered during research which was dated to the Hellenistic and Roman periods.

The auditorium of the Wadi Sabra theatre had a diameter of about 39 metres and was made up of eleven rows of seating which could have been occupied by 500-800 people (**Fig. 180**). However, only a section for about 150 people has survived to our times. The orchestra had a diameter of about 22 metres and some researchers believe that it could also have been used as a water tank. Above the auditorium, the remains of an imposing wall are visible, behind which a reservoir was situated. Water was transported to it via channels cut into the rock above. Both the theatre itself and the connected water supply system have been dated to the 1st century CE.

Almost directly opposite the theatre, we can see the remains of one of the dams which once surrounded the valley. They both served to collect water and at the same time to prevent possible flooding in periods of heavy rain.

About fifty metres further on, on the right (western) side of the wadi, are the remains of the 'acropolis' (**Fig. 181**). It is easy to identify them thanks to the enormous amount of ashlar blocks which remain from the destroyed

Fig. 180 – The Theatre in Wadi Sabra.

Fig. 181 – Ruins of buildings on the 'acropolis' of Wadi Sabra.

ancient buildings. Amongst the rubble, it is easy to spot Nabataean capitals, drum columns and elements of architectonic decoration (**Fig. 182**). Heading towards the acropolis, we can also observe further remains of the walls that once demarcated the valley.

Three small-scale archaeological surveys were carried out on the area of the acropolis in the 1990s. These confirmed the existence here of a small but

Fig. 182 – Fragment of an architectural decoration of the Nabataean temple.

Fig. 183 – The Oasis in the Wadi Sabra.

richly decorated Nabataean temple, which was dated to the 1st century BCE. During research, part of a marble statue of Aphrodite (of the *Anadyomene* type) was discovered, as well as a series of architectonic elements that would have once adorned the temple.

At the peak of the acropolis, we have the opportunity to admire the small oasis below (which is built around a small spring) in all its glory **(Fig. 183)**. It provides a sight for sore eyes with its luscious greenery backed by the reddish rock and yellow sand lying at the bottom of the wadi. It has not yet been established what type of settlement was found in the Wadi Sabra, although it has been suggested that it could have been a caravan station, a craft centre (suggested by the presence of kilns for smelting metal), a small sanctuary or even the winter residence of the Nabataean king (the Wadi Sabra is located about 100 metres below the level of Petra and enjoys a more clement climate). It is most likely, however, that a small independent settlement once stood here, which formed a southern suburb of Petra.

After seeing all that the Wadi Sabra has to offer and taking a suitable amount of rest, we return along exactly the same route which we took to get here.

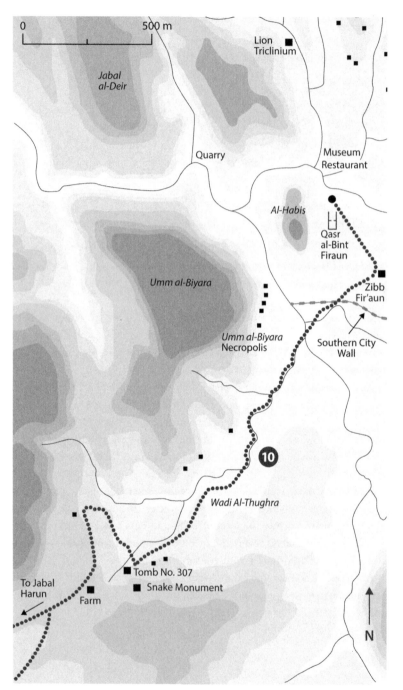

Fig. 184 – Trail No. 10.

TRAIL 10

Jabal al-Nabi Haroon (Fig. 184)

This is another trail for the more experienced tourist. As was the case with the route to the Wadi Sabra, we need a good deal of time for this journey (about five to six hours from central Petra) and a good sense of direction. The goal of this excursion is the highest rock elevation within the Petra area, Jabal Haroon, which rises to a height of 1,350 metres above sea level. We are also highly unlikely to meet other tourists on this trail, but the beautiful views which will accompany us both during the climb and the following descent will reward us for our strenuous efforts. We will also have the possibility to visit a 14th century mosque standing at the summit, which is alleged to be the final resting place of Aaron, the brother of Moses. In order to enter it, however, we will have to ask for the key from a guard living close to the trail to the peak. We must also remember that this is a holy site for Muslims and that we must therefore wear suitable clothing and behave appropriately.

As was the case with the previous trail, it is absolutely essential to wear good walking shoes and to take a mobile phone to summon assistance should you get into difficulty. Over the course of the nearly two hour climb to the summit, it is necessary to take frequent breaks and to consume plenty of water, so as not to become dehydrated (this is most important in the summer months). For this reason, a suitable amount of supplies must be taken, especially water (a bare minimum of three litres per person) as there will be no opportunity to replenish stocks during the trip.

The trail begins at the temple of Qasr al-Bint Firaun in the centre of Petra. We then follow the same path as Trail 9 as far as the 'farm'.

On reaching the plateau behind the 'farm', we soon pass the tents of a Bedouin family to our left. This family possesses the keys to the mosque found at the summit.

After expressing a desire to visit the mosque, we must expect to be accompanied by another person for the remainder of our journey. This does have its benefits, as the person will serve as our guide and we will therefore not be in danger of losing our way. It must be remembered, however, that for both the opportunity to enter the mosque and for being led to the summit of Jabal Haroon, we will be asked for a 'baksheesh' (voluntary donation) of about twenty to thirty Jordanian dinars. It is also sometimes the case that the person possessing the key to the mosque is living at the peak itself, close to the excavations of the Finnish archaeological mission. In this scenario, we will undoubtedly be invited to take tea and then led to the

Fig. 185 – Jabal al-Nabi Haroon.

mosque. *The baksheesh in this case would be between ten and twenty Jordanian dinars (depending on the size of the group).*

Continuing on, we take a path for off-road vehicles which runs off to the right, in the direction of the now visible summit of Jabal Haroon **(Fig. 185)**.

The way at first descends a little, but soon, after crossing the Wadi Waqit, it starts to go upwards once again. After a short while, we should see a path

heading in the direction of Jabal Haroon, which is marked by an illegible metal sign. It is relatively clearly visible, so we should not have any difficulty seeing it. From this place, we can also turn our attention to a rock formation (in the distance to the right (west)) which looks very much like the head of … Julius Caesar **(Fig. 186)**.

If we miss the trail, the worst thing that can happen is merely a slightly longer walk along the off-road vehicle track which circles Jabal Haroon and leads to its northern foot, from whence the next path takes us to the summit.

Fig. 186 – Rock 'head' of Julius Caesar.

Fig. 187 – The 'left' path leading up Mount Aaron.

If we do manage to take the correct path, it begins with a strenuous ascent. At one point, we come to a fork. The path leading left **(Fig. 187)** takes us to the foot of Jabal Haroon via a somewhat circuitous route, passing through the excavations being carried out by the Finnish archaeological mission. The path leading right **(Fig. 188)**, however, leads us directly to a small plateau, from where the final ascent to the summit begins.

Fig. 188 – The 'right' path leading up Mount Aaron.

Fig. 189 – Nabataean cistern.

When beginning this final climb, we should not miss the rare opportunity to see a still functioning Nabataean cistern **(Fig. 189)**. It is a very original construction with a ceiling held up by stone arches. After a short climb

Fig. 190 – Rock stairs leading to the summit of Mount Aaron.

(Fig. 190) of about five to ten minutes (mainly on steps), we reach the peak of Jabal Haroon.

The views, which are best enjoyed from the roof of the mosque, are incredible. To the east is the Wadi Araba and further on the Negev Desert. Looking north, we see the rocks surrounding the valley of Petra and the village of Wadi Musa situated behind. Amongst these rocks, we can discern the magnificent ed-Deir (the Monastery) and the large plateau in front of it **(Fig. 191)**.

To the south-west, the rocks surrounding the Wadi Sabra are visible and below, on the previously mentioned small plateau, we can see the remains of a Byzantine Pilgrimage Centre **(Fig. 192)**, which was con-

Fig. 191 – Ed-Deir among the rocks. View from Jabal Haroon.

structed on a site previously occupied by a Nabataean temple. Archaeological excavations have been carried out here since 1997 by archaeologists of the University of Helsinki (Finland), led by Zbigniew Fiema. Unfortunately,

Fig. 192 – Byzantine pilgrimage centre.

since archaeological work is still ongoing, the excavation site has not yet been opened to the public. For this reason, it is best to observe this area from the peak of Jabal Haroon.

Over the course of excavation work, it has been established that a Nabataean sanctuary was originally located on this site (in the western part of the excavation), the beginnings of which date to the 1ˢᵗ century BCE. In the second half of the 4ᵗʰ century CE, the site was increasingly connected to the death of Aaron, the brother of Moses, who passed away during the Israelites journey to the Promised Land. At the end of the 5ᵗʰ century CE, the Byzantine Church of Saint Aaron (in the eastern part of the excavation) was erected, as well as a whole monasterial complex, which was constructed due to the more and more commonly undertaken pilgrimage to Aaron's supposed final resting place.

The mosque found at the summit was built in the 14ᵗʰ century on the same location as an earlier building **(Fig. 193)**. As has already been mentioned, it is traditionally believed to be the resting place of Moses' brother, Aaron, who

Fig. 193 – Mosque on the top of Jabal Haroon.

Fig. 194 – The cenotaph of the prophet Aaron.

is considered to have been one of the prophets by Muslims. The modest interior contains just one room, in the centre of which a large pillar stands, which holds up the ceiling. On one of the walls opposite the entrance is a cenotaph of the prophet Aaron **(Fig. 194)**. Meanwhile, in one of the corners of the room, there are stairs leading to an underground crypt. It is worth examining the slab in the wall over the entrance with its extremely beautiful Arabic inscription, as well as the walls of the mosque, which were constructed using elements taken from earlier Nabataean and Byzantine buildings.

After seeing all that Jabal Haroon has to offer and taking a suitable rest, we return along exactly the same route which we took to get here.

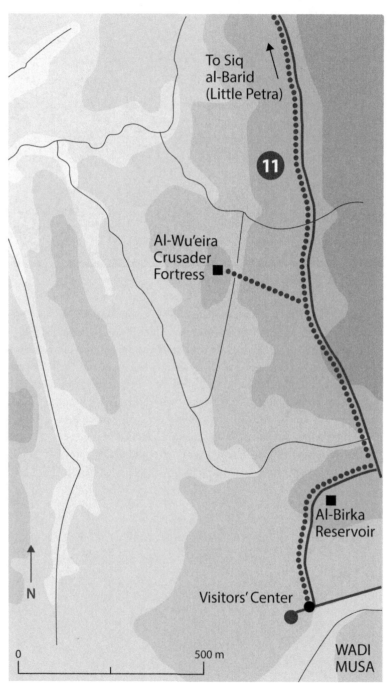

To Siq
al-Barid
(Little Petra)

11

Al-Wu'eira
Crusader
Fortress

Al-Birka
Reservoir

Visitors' Center

N

WADI
MUSA

0   500 m

Fig. 195 – Trail No. 11.

Al Wu'eira and Siq al-Barid (Little Petra) (Fig. 195)

This trail requires some kind of means of transportation. Without it, you will be forced into a lengthy walk along a tarmac road between the village of Wadi Musa and Siq al-Barid. In possession of a car, the trail will not take any longer than two hours. Walking, however, would require another four hours, as the two sites are about ten kilometres distant from each other. On the journey, you will witness the remains of a crusader fortress, a small gorge with several rock façades and (most interestingly) a room with a preserved fresco on its wall. In addition, you can familiarise yourself with the results of an archaeological investigation into the Neolithic site of Beidha, one of the earliest settlements in the whole of the Near East.

Do not forget to have your entrance ticket to Petra at hand, as both in al-Wu'eira and Siq al-Barid, we may meet guards who ask us to present it.

The trail begins at the tourist centre. The tarmac road from here leads to the north alongside the parking lot. At the nearby crossroads, we have to turn left towards the village of Beidha. After about 500 metres, we see the ruins of the Crusader Fortress **(Fig. 196)** at the top of al-Wu'eira to our left (west). Archaeological research on this site has been conducted for over fif-

Fig. 196 – Crusader Fortress at al-Wu'eira.

teen years by an expedition from the University of Florence (Italy) under the direction of Guido Vanini.

Turning towards the ruins, we come to a stone bridge which crosses over one of the deep rock gorges. After the bridge, we come to a rock-cut station used by guards in the Middle Ages **(Fig. 197)**. On passing this, we find ourselves inside the fortress itself.

Fig. 197 – Guardroom just after the stone bridge leading to the fortress of al-Wu'eira.

Unfortunately, the fortress today takes the form of a massive heap of rubble. The only areas worth visiting are the remains of the keep (partly restored by Italian archaeologists), the north and west towers and the remains of the church which lay between them, where Italian archaeologists have discovered rock-cut tombs below the floor of the main nave **(Fig. 198)**. Whilst studying the rocks around the fortress, a careful observer will also notice Nabataean traces in the form of cut steps, altars and votive niches.

After another one-and-a-half kilometres along the main road, we find ourselves in a place boasting a magnificent panorama of Petra between the peaks of al-Khubtha and Umm al-Biyara **(Fig. 199)**. In the distance, we can even make out Jabal Haroon with the albescent dome of its mosque at the peak. Continuing our journey, we pass a village where Bedouins of the Bdul tribe have been resettled and, after about six kilometres, we reach a crossroads where we must turn left (west).

After about another 600 metres, we come to the entrance of Siq al-Barid, also known as Little Petra. Siq al-Barid is something like the equivalent of

Fig. 198 – The remains of a church in the fortress of al-Wu'eira.

the Wadi Sabra (which lies to the south of Petra). A small settlement was probably located here, which would have been part of the northern suburbs of the capital of the Nabataeans. Before we enter the gorge itself **(Fig. 200)**,

Fig. 199 – Panorama of Petra from the road to Siq al-Barid.

Fig. 200 – The entrance to Siq al-Barid with Tomb No. 846 on the right.

we can admire the magnificent façade of the simple Roman Temple type Tomb 846 to our right. It has remained in surprisingly good condition up to our times. Two pillars made up of pilasters and quarter columns completed by Nabataean capitals support its Ionic entablature with a triangular gable. The frame of the entrance differs from the norm in that it is topped by a semicircular gable which stands above a Doric entablature. Opposite the tomb are two rock-cut rooms, one of which was used as a biclinium. Its unusual benches were cut at the bottom of the back and one of the side walls.

We now pass through a narrow crevice to reach the first 'courtyard'. Its most eye-catching feature is the façade of Temple 847 (in the *templum in antis* style), which is cut into rock to the left (south) **(Fig. 201)**. It should be noted that, although it has an entablature supported by columns and outer columns topped by magnificent Nabataean capitals, the façade lacks a gable. This is reminiscent of the Garden Temple found in Petra in the upper part of the Wadi Farasa.

Below this, we can see a rock-cut room which acts as a cistern by collecting water flowing down through channels cut into the rocks above. To the left, above the recess with a circular 'window', two traditional Nabataean betyls have been cut, undoubtedly symbolising the gods worshipped in the temple situated above.

After covering another 100 metres, another 'courtyard' opens out before us with rock-cut rooms and elements of a water collection system. Firstly, to the right, we see three triclinia with façades which would have once been

Fig. 201 – Facade of Temple No. 847 in Siq al-Barid.

decorated by pilasters. Opposite the last of these is another triclinium, next to which we can observe another underground cistern cut into the rock, as well as the channels supplying it with water.

Above is the most famous room of the whole of Siq al-Barid, Biclinium 849. Its walls are decorated with colourful frescos **(Fig. 202)** and we enter it via stairs situated to its left. The biclinium, similarly to the previously

Fig. 202 – Biclinium No. 849.

described one (at the entrance to the gorge), contains benches cut at the bottom of its side (eastern) and back (southern) walls. A large, curved, arch-shaped niche has also been cut into the back wall. On this wall are frescos of red paint on a cream background. This is reminiscent of the early phase of the Pompeiian II style, when frescos imitated the rock slabs (most often marble) of the wall's surface.

The most interesting, however, are the frescos on the curve of the back niche **(Fig. 203)**. They present grapevine creepers amongst which are numerous birds and at least three mythological characters: Pan playing the flute, Eros drawing his bow and Eros holding an undetermined object in his hand. According to the latest determination of F. Zayadine, the frescos date to the 1st century CE.

Fig. 203 – Frescos on the wall of Biclinium No. 849.

At the entrance to the biclinium, we should also pay attention to the small niche on the right, in which a small, rectangular betyl of several centimetres was cut. Opposite the biclinium, on the left, rock-cut steps leading to one of the area's high places are visible.

Continuing on, we come to a third 'courtyard', behind which we can see a narrow rock crevice which climbs upwards. After an ascent of several minutes, we come to a place where a beautiful view of the wide valley running from here towards the Wadi Araba extends. After a short rest (you can take advantage of the pleasant 'cafeteria' here to drink some tea or coffee), we return back the same way we came.

Fig. 204 – Neolithic settlement (in the distance) in the Wadi Beidha.

Those who are interested can also make a further trip to Beidha, where one of the oldest settlements in the world (dating to the Neolithic period) was once located **(Fig. 204)**. In order to get here we must take a road to the south which is intended for off-road vehicles. After a short while, the road turns to the east in the direction of a wide valley leading to the Wadi Araba. We continue our walk until we see an enclosed excavation site to the right (north) at the foot of a rock.

This place was investigated by Diana Kirkbridge for eight seasons between 1958 and 1983. As a result, the settlement has been dated to between 7000 and 6500 BCE (the Pre-Pottery Neolithic B period). Remains have also been discovered here dating to the times of 'Natufian Culture', which developed across the Near East between 10,000 and 9000 BCE.

Upon entering the excavation site, we can immediately see reconstructions of the kind of huts which would have been lived in during the Neolithic Period. Further along are the original remains of circular and rectangular rooms which would have been occupied by humans at this time. It is a pity, however, that they are not better protected, as in a few decades the place could fall into complete ruin.

After visiting the Neolithic village, we return to the car park in front of Siq al-Barid and take the same way back to the tourist centre on which we came.

Fig. 205 – Nabataean 'Horned' Capital.

GLOSSARY

Acanthus – A genus of herbaceous plants growing in the Mediterranean region and used as a decorative motif on Corinthian capitals.

Acroterion – In ancient architecture, a decorative element in the form of a figure, bas-relief or ornament which adorns an apex and/or the lower corners of a triangular gable of a temple or other building.

Adyton – The holiest part of a Greek temple which only priests may enter.

Aedicule – A niche framed by two columns or pilasters bearing an entablature and pediment.

Anta – A pillar in a Greek temple which forms the end of a protruding side wall, thereby creating a vestibule.

Apodyterium – A room in Roman baths used for changing.

Apse – A semi-circular room or recess.

Architrave – In ancient architecture, the lowest part of the entablature. It lies directly atop the capitals of the columns and below a tryglyph-metope (Doric order) or continuous (Ionic and Corinthian orders) frieze.

Arcosolium – An arched niche carved into rock.

Atrium – An open courtyard surrounded by a colonnaded covered walkway. Found in Roman houses and in front of Byzantine churches, often with a cistern below it.

Attic – The storey above the main entablature, often containing dwarf pilasters, reliefs or inscriptions.

Betyl – A rectangular stele carved in a relief or in the form of a portable idol and often placed in a niche. In Aramaic, the word 'betyl' means 'house of god'. The Nabataeans used the betyl to represent deities.

Biclinium – A room with two benches designed for dining, sometimes as part of a funeral.

Bouleuterion – In ancient Greece, the seat of the city council (boule) and the place where they met.

Caldarium – A room in Roman baths which contained a pool of hot water.

Capital – The top element of the column or pilaster. It is often a form of decoration.

Cavea – The viewing area or auditorium in Roman theatres, most often semi-circular. The equivalent of the Greek 'theatron'.

Cella – In ancient architecture, the most important, central room of a temple, which normally contained a statue of the god to whom the temple was dedicated.

Cenotaph – A kind of symbolic grave dedicated to a person buried elsewhere.

Columbarium – A tomb with niches for urns containing ashes, sometimes used as a dovecote.

Cornice – In classical architecture, the upper element of an entablature above the architrave and frieze.

Crowstep – Crenellations with stepped sides, used as decoration on Nabataean tombs.

Doric frieze – A frieze of the Doric order decorated with alternating triglyphs and metopes.

Dwarf pilaster – A small pilaster.

Entablature – In classical architecture, the horizontal structure above the capitals. It consists of an architrave, frieze and cornice.

Exedra – In ancient architecture, a semi-circular, open niche.

Fascia – A broad flat band used in classical architecture.

Frieze – The middle element of a classical entablature located between the architrave and cornice.

Frigidarium – A room in Roman baths which contained a cold pool.

Hypocaust – The heating system in Roman baths. It blew hot air in from underneath the floor (which was supported by pillars).

Ionic frieze – A frieze of the Ionic order. It could be flat or decorated with ornaments or figural depictions.

In situ – In its original location.

Metope – In the Doric order, a flat stone slab, sometimes covered with relief decoration, positioned between two tryglyphs.

Monopteros – A round building without walls comprising a circular colonnade supporting a conical roof.

Narthex – In Early Christian architecture, a kind of transverse lobby fronting the entrance to a basilica.

Nave – A central space in church with two aisles, often separated by colonnades.

Nephesh – In Semitic languages, it means 'soul' and relates most frequently to commemorative stelae. In Nabataean art, it usually takes the form of a cone or obelisk standing on a rectangular or cylindrical base. The Nabataeans used the nephesh as a way to remember the dead.

Niche – A recess in a wall for a statue or other ornament, often rectangular or semicircular and sometimes arched.

Nymphaeum – In ancient Greece, it was initially a natural site (most often based around a spring) where nymphs were worshipped. In later times, however, it possessed architectural elements. In ancient Rome, it was a fountain (nymphaion), most often with monumental, architectonic framing, from which water (transported via pipes) emerged.

Odeon – A small theatre, sometimes roofed, where music or recitation contests were held.

Orchestra – A circular or semi-circular stage intended for the chorus in an ancient theatre.

Palmette – An ornament somewhat resembling a palm-leaf.

Pastophorium – In early churches, two small rooms located on either side of the presbytery.

Pediment – In classical architecture, the structure crowning the front of the building. It often contains a sculpture in its tympanum.

Peristyle – In ancient architecture, a courtyard surrounded by a columned portico (colonnade).

Pilaster – In ancient architecture, a flat pillar adjacent to a wall with a base and a capital, most often with a decorative rather than a constructive role.

Praecinctio – In Roman theatres, a horizontal passageway between sectors (cuneus) of the viewing area. The equivalent of a Greek diazoma.

Pronaos – In Greek temples, the lobby in front of the cella.

Propylaea – In Greek architecture, a monumental gate with several passageways separated by rows of columns.

Pulpitum – In Roman theatres, a platform which played the role of a stage on which actors performed. The equivalent of the Greek proskenion.

Pylon – Towers that flanked the entrance to an Egyptian temple.

Relief – A sculpture or ornament projecting from a background.

Scenae Frons – In Roman theatres, a stage building providing the background for the stage on which actors performed. The equivalent of the Greek skene.

Stele – A stone burial slab, normally covered in relief decoration or inscriptions.

Stucco – Plaster or calcareous cement render, plain or modelled.

Temenos – An enclosed area used in cult worship. A sacred precinct.

Templum in antis (In Latin = Temple between antae) – In ancient architecture, a small, rectangular temple with an entry on its shorter side through a lobby located between antae.

Tepidarium – In Roman baths, a room with a warm pool.

Therme – A complex of public baths in a Roman city used for bathing, social gatherings and during leisure time.

Tetrastyle – A building with four columns in its façade.

Tholos – In ancient architecture, a circular building.

Torus – A large, semi-circular, convex moulding.

Triclinium – A room with three benches designed for dining, sometimes as part of a funeral.

Triglyph – In the Doric order, an element of the entablature in the shape of a four-sided slab. It has two vertical grooves that divide it into three parts.

Tympanum – The triangular, interior area of a gable in a temple or other building, often decorated with bas-reliefs.

SELECTED BIBLIOGRAPHY

Augé Ch., Dentzer J. M., *Petra. The Rose-Red City*, London 2000.

Bachmann W., Watzinger C., Wiegand T., *Petra, Wissenschaftliche Veröffentlichungen des Deutsch-Türkischen Denkmalschutz – Kommandos*, Heft 3, Lipsk 1921.

Bedal L-A., *The Petra Pool-Complex. A Hellenistic Paradeisos in the Nabataean Capital*, Gorgias Press 2004.

Bini M., Bertocci S. (eds.), *Castelli di pietre. Aspetti formali e materiali dei castelli crociati nell'area di Petra in Transgiordania*, Firenze 2004.

Bowersock G., *Roman Arabia*, Harvard University Press 1983.

Browning I., *Petra*, London 1982.

Brünnow R. E., Domaszewski A. von, *Die Provincia Arabia*, Vol. I-III, Strasburg 1904–1909.

Burckhardt J. L., *Travels in Syria and Holy Land*, London 1822.

Dalman G., *Petra und seine Felsheiligtümer*, Lipsk 1908.

Dalman G., *Neue Petra Forschungen*, Lipsk 1912.

Fiema Z. T., *The Petra Church*, Amman 2001.

Flavius Josephus, *The Works of Flavius Josephus*, Translated by William Whiston, A.M. Auburn and Buffalo John E. Beardsley, 1895.

Frosen J., Fiema Z. T., *Petra – A City Forgotten and Rediscovered*, Helsinki 2002.

Glueck N., *Deities and Dolphins*, London 1966.

Grawehr M., *Petra – Ez Zantur IV*, Terra Archaeologica VI, Mainz 2010.

Hammond P. C., *The Excavation of the Main Theatre at Petra, 1961–1962*, London 1965.

Hammond P. C., *The Nabataeans – Their History, Culture and Archaeology*, Studies in Mediterranean Archaeology 37, Stockholm 1973.

Hammond P. C., *The Temple of the Winged Lions, Petra, Jordan, 1973–1990*, Utah 1991.

Healey J. F., *The Religion of the Nabataeans. A Conspectus*, Leiden 2001.

Irby C. L., Mangles J., *Travels in Egypt and Nubia, Syria and Asia Minor during the years 1817 and 1818*, London 1823.

Joukowsky M. S., *Petra Great Temple, vol. I-II*, Providence 1998-2007.

Keller D., Grawehr M., *Petra – Ez Zantur III*, Terra Archaeologica V, Mainz 2006.

Khouri R. G., Petra. *A Guide to the capital of the Nabataeans*, London-New York 1986.

Kolb B., Schmid S., Stucky R., *Petra – Ez Zantur I*, Terra Archaeologica II, Mainz 1996.

Kolb B., Schmid S., *Petra – Ez Zantur II*, Terra Archaeologica IV, Mainz 2000.

Laborde L., *Voyage d'Arabie Petree*, Paris 1830.

Lindner M. (ed.), *Petra, Neue Ausgrabungen und Entdeckungen*, München, Bad Windsheim 1986.

Lindner M. (ed.), *Petra und das Königreich der Nabatäer*, München, Bad Windsheim 1989.

Markoe G. (ed.), *Petra Rediscovered. Lost City of the Nabataeans*, London-New York 2003.

McKenzie J. S., *The Architecture of Petra*, Oxford 1990.

Mouton M., Schmid S.G. (eds.), *Men on the Rocks. The Formation of Nabataean Petra*, Berlin 2013.

Musil A., *Arabia Petraea, vol. II, Edom*, Wien 1907.

Nehmé L., Wadeson L. (eds.), *The Nabataeans in Focus: Current Archaeological Research at Petra*, Supplement to the Proceedings of the Seminar for Arabian Studies 42, Oxford 2012.

Netzer E., *Nabatäische Architektur*, Mainz am Rhein 2003.

Patrich J., *The Formation of Nabatean Art*, Jerusalem 1990.

Petra. Begleitbuch zur Ausstellung «Petra – Wunder in der Wüste. Auf den Spuren von J. L. Burckhardt alias Scheich Ibrahim», Antikenmuseum Basel und Sammlung Ludwig, Basel 2012.

Politis K. D. (ed.), *The World of the Nabataeans*, Franz Steiner Verlag 2007.

Rababeh S. M., *How Petra was Built. An analysis of the construction techniques of the Nabataean freestanding buildings and rock-cut monuments in Petra, Jordan*, BAR International Series 1460, Oxford 2005.

Roberts D., *The Holy Land*, vol.V, London 1849.

Strabo, ed. H. L. Jones, *The Geography of Strabo*. Cambridge, Mass., Harvard University Press, London, William Heinemann, Ltd. 1924.

Taylor J., *Petra and the Lost Kingdom of the Nabataeans*, Harvard University Press 2002.

Zayadine F. (ed.), *Petra and the Caravan Cities*, Amman 1990.

Printed in Great Britain
by Amazon

15964970R00120